Bringing Teachers to
the History Museum

AMERICAN ALLIANCE OF MUSEUMS

The American Alliance of Museums has been bringing museums together since 1906, helping to develop standards and best practices, gathering and sharing knowledge, and providing advocacy on issues of concern to the entire museum community. Representing more than 35,000 individual museum professionals and volunteers, institutions, and corporate partners serving the museum field, the Alliance stands for the broad scope of the museum community.

The American Alliance of Museums' mission is to champion museums and nurture excellence in partnership with its members and allies.

Books published by AAM further the Alliance's mission to make standards and best practices for the broad museum community widely available.

American
Alliance of
Museums

Bringing Teachers to the History Museum

A Guide to Facilitating Teacher Professional Development

Edited by Lora Cooper, Linnea Grim,
and Gary Sandling

ROWMAN & LITTLEFIELD
Lanham • Boulder • New York • London

Published by Rowman & Littlefield
An imprint of The Rowman & Littlefield Publishing Group, Inc.
4501 Forbes Boulevard, Suite 200, Lanham, Maryland 20706
www.rowman.com

86-90 Paul Street, London EC2A 4NE

British Library Cataloguing in Publication Information Available

Library of Congress Cataloging-in-Publication Data

Names: Cooper, Lora, editor. | Grim, Linnea, editor. | Sandling, Gary, editor.
Title: Bringing teachers to the history museum : a guide to facilitating teacher
    professional development / edited by Lora Cooper, Linnea Grim, and Gary
    Sandling.
Description: Lanham : Rowman & Littlefield ; [Washington, D.C.] : American
    Alliance of Museums, [2022] | Includes bibliographical references and index.
Identifiers: LCCN 2022005264 (print) | LCCN 2022005265 (ebook) |
    ISBN 9781538145456 (cloth) | ISBN 9781538145463 (paperback) | ISBN
    9781538145470 (ebook)
Subjects: LCSH: Teachers—Training of—United States. | Historical museums—
    United States. | Museums—Educational aspects—United States. | Museum
    outreach programs—United States. | Public history—United States.
Classification: LCC LB1715 .B725 2022 (print) | LCC LB1715 (ebook) | DDC
    370.71/1—dc23/eng/20220421
LC record available at https://lccn.loc.gov/2022005264
LC ebook record available at https://lccn.loc.gov/2022005265

Dedicated to all of the teachers who have inspired us.

Contents

Acknowledgments

We created this book for museum education practitioners because we are dedicated to offering the best possible professional development experience for our most valuable adult constituency: classroom teachers. Teachers have a tremendous responsibility, and we want to support them in their work as effectively as possible, learning from them even as we share the tools, sources, and understandings of our historic site. Teachers deserve the respect and care fitting for the emotional and intellectual work they do. It is our greatest hope that this volume may assist in your own efforts in serving the needs of teachers. The editors know that all of the contributors to this volume share that value, as do the more than forty museum educators from fifteen historic sites and museums who met at the Fred W. Smith Library at Mount Vernon on September 5 and 6, 2019, to exchange best practices, strategies, and evaluation tools. This book is one outcome of that effort, as is the companion website: teacherinsites. org. We extend special thanks to Tim Patterson (Temple University College of Education and Human Development), Kristin Gallas (Tsongas Industrial History Center), Rhonda Watton (Templeton Middle School, Sussex, Wisconsin), and Sherri Sklarwitz (Tisch College of Civic Life, Tufts University), who provided critical feedback to the contributors.

Funding for these efforts was made possible through two grants from the Institute for Museum and Library Services (IMLS), for which the editors served as project managers and coordinators. An IMLS National Leadership Grant (MG-10-15-0095) funded the development of a Q-sort evaluation tool for historic sites and a Museums for America Grant (MA-10-19-0617) allowed us to produce the manuscript for this publication. We are also grateful to the American Alliance of Museums and Rowman & Littlefield for seeing the work through to publication.

Finally, we are grateful to all who share in this work with us.

Introduction

Lora Cooper

This book's origins began in 2014 with a question: What do teachers learn at professional development programs at historic sites and museums (HSM)? This question encompassed several others: How are teachers influenced in their thinking and classroom practices by an individual program? How are the collective efforts of place-based professional development programs affecting classroom education across the country? Furthermore, how do HSM fit into the larger landscape of teacher professional development (TPD)? What are we positioned to offer, and how does this work support our institutions? At the root of these questions was a desire to know the lasting impact of TPD at HSM. We wanted to know the value of our programs for the edification of our teachers and staff, but we also wanted to demonstrate that value to funders, leadership, and internal stakeholders.

A National Leadership Grant from the Institute of Museum and Library Services (MG 10-15-0095-15) funded a three-year evaluation project that produced actionable data and constructive feedback. Using Q-Methodology (see chapter 5), researchers collected data from teachers attending summer programs at Thomas Jefferson's Monticello, Mystic Seaport Museum, and George Washington's Mount Vernon. As HSM educators learned about teachers as a distinctive audience, we also learned about ourselves as teacher educators. A handful of deceptively simple takeaways helped us transform our programs through practical changes that led to deeper learning:

1. **Teachers as passionate professionals**. The combination of personal and professional motivations, especially when traveling without students or family, shapes teachers' perceptions of on-site learning experiences. Teachers choose to attend site-based TPD because they want to be there and are passionate history lovers; they also never stop thinking about their students. All their learning is filtered through the question: How can I share this with my students?

2. **The power of place**. The effect of being "in the room where it happened" is intrinsic to HSM and, therefore, what they can offer to teachers. As teachers come from classrooms across the nation, history can be brought to life through the spaces and objects that they may only get to spend a brief time talking about in a survey course. However, this proximity doesn't create meaningful learning on its own. Taking teachers behind the scenes into the work of public history—be it archaeology, exhibit design, document analysis, or school program resources—helps them make meaning of a site in ways that can translate to deeper student learning experiences back in the classroom.

3. **An inquiry-driven approach to TPD**. Rather than offering teachers an all-you-can-eat "content buffet," presenting them seemingly less content with more opportunities to process creates learning experiences that stick. Inquiry and the skills of "being a historian" shape current learning standards; modeling inquiry for and with teachers bolsters the historical thinking skills they share with students.

4. **Peer-to-peer learning**. Teachers learning from one another enables participants to reflect upon content and connect it with their classroom needs. This requires time during the program that, at first glance on a schedule, can appear unstructured, wasted, or simply social. However, once teachers return to the daily demands of the classroom the opportunities to translate their learning into student learning experiences are far fewer. Teachers are excellent translators and scavengers, especially when collaborating with one another. Facilitating time in which they can process with one another bolsters teachers' connections to the program and institution.

These takeaways call for TPD at HSM to be driven by inquiry and collaboration. While there is still more to learn before answering our precipitating questions, our findings offer transferable takeaways that can strengthen TPD at HSM and demonstrate its value. The chapters that follow draw upon this research and the experiential expertise of educators from multiple fields with the aim of articulating fieldwide standards for creating broad, long-term efficacy in TPD programs at HSM. This book is a practical guide for enacting these principles from the conception to the evaluation of a program.

The shift in our research and work pivoted on a recognition that being a teacher educator requires a different set of skills than working with most other visitors, fulfilling the age-old trope of learning more about ourselves through our work than we did about our supposed subject. Learning more about ourselves—and what we could change—proved the key to better serving the educators we sought to support. Our own tour guide tendencies to share everything we know, and the temptation to present a highly polished museum experience, led us to model poor teaching practices. Instead, we needed to invite conversation. We were able to meet teachers' expectations in ways that were richer than they or we expected after educating ourselves on teaching standards and uncovering teacher attitudes through Q-Methodology. We could design sessions that encourage teachers looking for quick resources to engage deeply with content and still walk away with something ready to be used in the classroom. We could connect with teachers who would be happy to be left alone in our research libraries and help them keep sight of the breadth and scope of historical themes students are trying to comprehend. However, we grasped a fuller picture of how to meet teachers where they are, through the combined insights of their personal expectations revealed through evaluations and the professional needs articulated in field standards.

We also needed a richer understanding of what our own field of public history could offer teachers. History teachers—many of which are self-proclaimed nerds—are some of the most fun museum guests to observe in an exhibit or historic space. They light up with enthusiasm about spending time on-site with others who share their enthusiasm. This revitalization of teachers' love of history is valuable in and of itself when examining the worth of place-based teacher education. The work comes in helping teachers translate that engagement into meaningful understandings of history that they can then share with their students. For when they return to their classrooms, teaching is the task at hand. Public history's interdisciplinary work is a perfect companion to the historical thinking skills emphasized in standards of learning. Sharing history professionally is the process of developing reasoned and evidenced arguments. How was the format of a new exhibit decided upon? How do archaeologists decide where to dig? How was a school program activity developed? What new sources have been uncovered or are being newly considered? What sources are pointedly absent? The modern functions of the museum become as much a part of the lesson as what the museum preserves.

Public history is both adjacent to and a part of academic scholarship and formal education alike; museums are already part of a dynamic of shared authority and expertise. Therefore, inviting participating teachers to share their own insights further enriches their experience and the museum's understanding. Indeed, this models good teaching by asking teachers to be active participants rather than passive audience members. Teachers can and should be involved in identifying broad historical concepts and transferable skills, contextualizing no-longer-lived-in spaces, and investigating sources. Leveraging the excitement of being on-site into peer-to-peer learning allows teachers to construct historical knowledge and ask questions about the process through which that occurs. TPD at HSM can help teachers navigate the tension between conveying the nuances of historical narratives and distilling content into a means and quantity that is suited to their students' needs. These rich conversations build relationships between teachers and between teachers and sites. As one educator said on a return visit to Monticello with his students, "I didn't have a professional community before I came here, and now I do."

Our self-conception of the role of museum educators in TPD shifted not only through our evaluation process but also by surrounding world events. Our programs were shaped by the realities of teaching through the 2016 election, the 2017 events in Charlottesville, Virginia, and more. Teachers and HSM staff expressed an urgent need to engage students with difficult history. Since the conception of this book, COVID-19 has brought the move to virtual instruction; we have had a summer of Black Lives Matter protests, another election, and violent demonstrations of white supremacy. Museums operate with immense perceived authority, which is partly based in a misconception of neutrality.[1] We can leverage this perception to share highly relevant content and host essential conversations—if facilitators are prepared to do so. Teachers want to connect with history professionals, and their students want to have the difficult conversations. TPD at HSM can help educators explore the distinctions between history and memory, build critical analysis skills and media literacy, and more. Presenting reasoned and evidenced interpretations of history in which students can see themselves and their world is a more critical obligation than ever before. All of this is not to say that museums can, or should, be all things to all teachers. On the contrary, the research indicates the limitations of trying to share everything we have in a limited time. However, by starting with a rich understanding of teachers as a distinct audience and how our institutions can uniquely support their learning, museum educators can become better teacher educators. This reimagining of our roles and programs can help us understand *how* to share our content in ways that are meaningful for future implementation with students. A Mount Vernon teacher participant captured this shift perfectly when describing the site as "a place where history happened and is happening."

When the researchers highlighted that quote as indicative of the thinking of largest set of teachers in the evaluation, we felt that we'd done exactly what we'd set out to do. That pithy phrase reflects a rich engagement with content, an understanding of historical thinking, and a meaningful connection with the site. It embodies the likelihood of a long-standing relationship and meaningful engagement for years to come.

HOW TO USE THIS BOOK

Just as we found the most effective TPD to be collaborative in nature, both teacher-to-teacher and teacher-to-site staff, so too is this book. As TPD at HSM falls at the intersection of many fields of expertise, a thorough understanding of best practices requires the insights of each. Calling on both research and experience, the contributors to this book come from museum education, teacher education, museum leadership, and, of course, classroom education. We hope the efficacy of inquiry-driven programs, with the supporting research based as much in understanding teachers and teaching as it is in sites and their history, will translate to TPD in science and art museums and other similar institutions. However, for the purposes of this book, we have confined ourselves to the realm of HSM based on our research and experience.

This book is divided between theory (part I) and practice (part II); we hope you'll closely examine the understandings our findings are based around and then grab concrete tips and ideas from the practical portion.

We begin with a robust understanding of the theoretical frameworks for our practical takeaways. Our audience takes center stage as we consider who teachers are as learners and the processes they use to share content with their students. To look at how we help in that process, chapters are dedicated to teaching difficult topics and making interdisciplinary connections. We then examine the foundational research and the significance of evaluation. Then our attention shifts to building a robust program, beginning with how to set objectives that serve and align with your institution, how to explore different formats, including virtual, and how to make logistics contribute to successful learning experiences. Program facilitators will share their lessons learned on making the most of program recruitment, teacher-created products, and funding models. Finally, we'll take a look at how programs have implemented evaluation, how to use them wisely and on a manageable scale, and how to implement findings.

Beyond the binding of this book, further resources are available to you and your program. A group of museum educators who facilitate TPD, known as the Teacher InSites Collaborative, have come together to support one another and classroom educators. When presenting the precipitating research at the annual meetings of museum professional organizations, we found that informal gatherings of TPD facilitators were far more productive and were needed. Museum educators could don our teacher

educator hats and exchange ideas on everything from funding and application questions to how much social time was built into each of our
programs. These gatherings became the capstone of our research and the
groundwork for this book: Summit on Teacher Professional Development
at Historic Sites and Museums at Mount Vernon in September 2019. When
the COVID-19 pandemic began, this community became an (often frantic)
email chain, as each represented institution took TPD virtual via different
means and formats. Then we began regularly scheduled Zoom calls to
exchange ideas and check in on one another and the classroom teachers
we all seek to support. In 2021, some of these institutions joined together
to collaboratively host a series of virtual TPD workshops. At teacher-
insites.org, you'll find further samples of the work we've highlighted
in the following chapters, links to journal articles, and how to join the
collaborative.

In July 2021, we were once again able to welcome educators to an on-
site, in-person Monticello Teacher Institute. Their excitement was palp-
able, their questions honest, and their takeaways insightful. We hope this
book will do the same for your institution's TPD facilitators as we seek to
support classrooms together.

NOTE

1. La Tanya S. Autry and Mike Murawski, "Museums Are Not Neutral: We Are
Stronger Together," *Panorama: Journal of the Association of Historians of American Art*
5, no. 2 (2019), https://doi.org/10.24926/24716839.2277.

I

+

THEORY

1

Teachers as Learners

Stephanie van Hover

Teaching is, by its very nature, an incredibly complex endeavor. A study in the early twentieth century (*The Commonwealth Teacher Training Study*) attempted to capture all the actions or activities that teachers engage in, and the final list came in at more than a thousand items.[1] Research (and the lived experience of teachers) highlights the interactional, contextual nature of teaching and the need for constant decision-making, interpretation, reflection, and judgment—not to mention knowledge of subject matter and students. Knowledge of teaching is not static but involves lifelong learning, typically provided through professional development. Professional development offers the opportunity for teachers to be learners, to continue to develop their instructional practice, and, in turn, to enrich student learning opportunities. These learning experiences can take place in formal and informal settings, some mandated by a school or division, others self-selected by adult professionals seeking to enrich their knowledge.

So, the central question framing this chapter is: What does it mean for a teacher to be a learner? Furthermore: What does it mean to facilitate effective professional development for teachers as learners? While the field of teacher education (for both preservice and in-service teachers) continues to both debate and grapple with the "best" way to support teacher learning, I draw on work (both theoretical and research based) that I argue is relevant and useful to those working in historic sites and museums (HSM). The following sections briefly synthesize some key ideas from the fields of professional development, adult learning theory, and teacher education in order to generate actionable ideas for HSM educators.

Professional Development and Adult Learning Theory

As Husbands and Pendry observe, "All commentators take as the starting point the ultimate goal of professional development to be enhancing the quality of teaching and thereby the quality of learning by pupils"; but, they add, "once this rather obvious goal is stated, consensus of how to achieve this breaks down."[2] Implementation of professional development varies widely, and evidence suggests that a high percentage of professional development opportunities are ineffective and have little impact on teaching and learning.[3] Research does suggest that certain program design features (duration, topic, intensity, number of contact hours, learning activities, collective participation) are "unreliable predictors of program success"[4] and that, similarly, programs focused exclusively on building content knowledge in teachers have uneven effects on student learning. Despite this lack of clarity, professional development continues to be seen as the best opportunity to support teacher learning, foster effective teaching, and promote student learning.

So then, what to consider? Ideally, professional development is, as Kennedy argues, informed by a theory of action with two highly interactional components: (a) a problem of practice that the professional development providers seek to address; and (b) a clearly identified set of knowledge and strategies that provides teachers with new ways to address the problem of practice and enact new ideas in their particular classroom contexts.[5] Kennedy also observes that the problems of practice tend to emerge from five challenges that all teachers face: portraying the curriculum, enlisting student participation, exposing student thinking, containing student behavior, and accommodating personal needs.[6] Teachers learn best when professional development focuses explicitly on addressing these problems of practice. The challenge most relevant for HSM educators to address is that of "portraying the curriculum," in which teachers are deciding what and how to teach particular subject matter.

Another key consideration for planning professional development is that teachers are adult learners and, as such, bring a unique set of circumstances to the setting. There are multiple theories or assumptions about how adults learn, including one called "andragogy."[7] Andragogy, which has both proponents and critics, was first conceptualized in 1980 by Malcolm Knowles, who argued that *peda*gogy was child-focused and called for greater attention to the adult learner (hence, *andra*["man"]gogy). As Merriam and Beirema note, Knowles called for attention to process, that a professional development facilitator should set a "climate for learning that physically and psychologically respects adult learners and then involves the learners in the planning, delivery, and evaluation of their own learning."[8] Adult learners, according to Knowles, are more self-directed and ready to learn, can draw on life and work experiences to sense-make new information, are more problem-centered, and need to understand *why* they are learning something.[9]

In sum, we can learn from the literature on professional development and adult learning theory that professional development for teachers as learners should identify and address problems of practice and problem-based investigation; establish the reason or purpose for the learning experience; attend to positive classroom climate; emphasize learning by doing and collaboration; and respect and recognize the experiences and backgrounds that adult learners bring to a session. The actual process of teaching teachers (as adult learners) presents an additional challenge and can be informed by work in teacher education.

Teacher Education, Core Practices, and Modeling

Teacher education (the collective learning experiences for those who want to *become* teachers) as a field continues to debate the best approach to prepare effective teachers. That said, in recent years, a shared focus has emerged—"professional training on 'core' or 'high-leverage' practices of teaching,"[10] which are research-based instructional practices that are used frequently, have been shown to impact student achievement, reflect the complex nature of teaching and learning, and help teachers know their students.[11] There is no approved list of core practices that everyone agrees upon; rather, they can vary by content area or by organization. For example, TeachingWorks, at the University of Michigan[12] outlines nineteen "high-leverage practices," including "leading a group discussion, "eliciting and interpreting individual students' thinking," and "explaining and modeling content, practices, and strategies."[13] A content area example that is relevant to the work of historic sites and many museums is the field of history education. Brad Fogo identified core practices for history education: "[U]se historical questions; select and adapt historical sources; explain and connect historical content; model and support historical reading skills; employ historical evidence; use historical concepts; facilitate discussion of historical topics; model and support historical writing; assess student thinking about history."[14]

The professional training on these (and other) core practices involves: building teachers' background knowledge of subject matter; teacher educators "breaking apart" each practice to ensure that teachers understand the component parts (without becoming too granular); modeling the practice (by the instructor making thinking visible, or through video review); and providing students with the opportunity to plan for instruction and engage in small-group practice (with peer or instructor feedback). Ultimately, teachers enact the new skill in a P–12 context and, in an optimal setting, receive high-quality feedback and the opportunity to reflect and try again. An essential component is ensuring teachers understand the goal or purpose of each practice—the *why* and *when*—as well as *how* to implement the practice across varied, complex contexts.

What are the implications of this approach for museum educators and historic sites? That, rather than being everything to everyone, it is worthwhile to identify and explicitly model a core practice that lends itself to the experiences and resources unique to the museum or historic site *and* addresses a problem of practice meaningful to classroom teachers. For example, one focus for a historic site could be "employ historic evidence," which Fogo defines as "how the teacher uses and supports students in using, multiple forms of evidence . . . to develop and support historical claims and understand the connections between claims and evidence."[15] Professional development sessions would mirror the teacher education approach: (a) build background knowledge on a topic relevant to teachers and their students through interactive and experiential learning experiences; (b) identify, define, and "break apart" the practice of selecting historical evidence unique to the museum or historic site and relevant to the subject matter focus; (c) model the selection of evidence and how historians and experts analyze and understand evidence (connections between historic claims and evidence); (d) model how teachers could teach students to analyze historical evidence (perhaps drawing on scaffolds developed by Stanford History Education Group or the National Archives); (e) provide teachers with time to practice with each other; and (f) facilitate a debrief in which teachers reflect on how these approaches would work for their unique contextual circumstances and with their students.

Modeling involves demonstrating how the approach could be used in a P–12 setting *and* involves "making thinking visible"—in the sense of employing historic evidence, making visible how a teacher teaches students the steps of analysis, as well as how a historian would think about historical evidence. Including vignettes or case studies can also be helpful for adult learners to see the possibility of the approach and reflect on how they can translate new ideas into existing frameworks. And for the debrief, it's useful to consider Fogo's caution that although "teaching practices can be identified, learned, and practiced, they do not stand alone in classrooms" but are "filtered through a teacher's historical and historiographical content knowledge and selected, combined, and pursued in relation to specific groups of students in different learning environments."[16]

In sum, core practices do provide for a common language and a way to focus on specific instructional practices known to support students' learning; and they can be used to answer the *why* question and address a teaching challenge (portraying the curriculum). Whether content-neutral strategies from TeachingWorks or content-specific, core practices provide a useful way of thinking about structuring teacher learning and can be utilized not just in preservice but also in in-service teacher education (professional development) with adult learners.

Teachers as Learners: Implications for Professional Development

In this section, to conclude, I take key ideas from the sections above and generate what I hope is a helpful synthesis or summation of things to consider in order to support teachers as learners for educators in museums and historic sites.

> **Pre-session interest survey**: If resources permit, use an online form to distribute a pre-survey to get a sense of how your participants identify, the context in which they are teaching, and what they hope to learn from the professional development session (their *why*). The survey could also include a list of core practices and participants could identify those that they would like to learn more about.
>
> **Planning for content, purpose, and core practices**: Based on both the audience and the nature of the historic site or museum, identify the content knowledge *and* strategies associated with that content knowledge and associated resources. Rather than quantity, focus on quality. What core practice (singular!) can you connect to your experiential learning and subject matter knowledge? For example, are there historical sources you can feature, with an emphasis on how teachers can "employ historical evidence"? Also, articulate a clear purpose—that is, *why* the content and the strategies (or core practices) are important and will support student learning.
>
> **Climate for learning**: Whether in person or digital, as noted earlier, the climate or learning environment matters for teacher learning. How will participants get to know each other? Get to know the facilitator? How will the facilitator ensure all voices are heard? How are you drawing on the experience each learner brings to the session? How will you establish the reason for the session, the purpose, the learning objectives, the *why*?
>
> **Enacting the session (learn, practice, apply, reflect)**: Structure the session with a learner-centered framework: learn, practice, apply, reflect. Think about how participants will learn the content and the core practices—move beyond didactic presentation of content and focus on ways in which participants can engage with the ideas and with each other. Consider borrowing from practice-based teacher education, and develop sessions that build subject matter knowledge while also introducing and modeling a way in which to use the

unique resources of the museum or historic site. Provide opportunity for teachers to practice or apply what they have learned, and to give each other feedback and reflect on how the new learning can be applied in their specific teaching context. Participants could, if appropriate, engage in activities from the perspective of their students and then reflect together on ways in which they could adjust strategies for their students. In other words, museum educators model, other teachers model, and teachers get to participate as students.

Post-experience survey: The post-experience survey can assess participant satisfaction with the learning experience and solicit feedback but also include a reflective element in which participants identify what they learned and what they intend to use in the classroom.

In sum, the research suggests that structuring and implementing highly effective professional development sessions is challenging. The ideas presented here are intended to help museum educators focus on teachers as adult learners and consider the unique needs of teachers as learners. Supporting teachers as learners is an exciting way to affect the day-to-day experiences of students in P–12 classrooms by making museums and historic sites a part of learning.

NOTES

1. Francesca Forzani, "Understanding 'Core Practices' and 'Practice-Based' Teacher Education: Learning from the Past," *Journal of Teacher Education* 65, no. 2 (2014): 357.

2. Chris Husbands and Anna Pendry, "Continued Professional Development," in *History Teachers in the Making: Professional Learning*, eds. Anna Pendry, Chris Husbands, James Arthur, and Joe Davison (Buckingham, England: Open University Press, 1998), 125.

3. Mary Kennedy, "How Does Professional Development Improve Teaching?" *Review of Educational Research* 86, no. 4 (2016): 945; Stephanie van Hover, "Professional Development of Social Studies Teachers," in *Handbook of Research in Social Studies*, eds. Linda S. Levstik and Cynthia A. Tyson (New York: Routledge, 2018), 352; Stephanie van Hover and David Hicks, "History Teacher Preparation and Professional Development," in *International Handbook of History Teaching and Learning*, eds. Scott Alan Metzger and Laurent McArthur Harris (Hoboken, NJ: Wiley-Blackwell, 2018), 391.

4. Kennedy, "How Does Professional Development Improve Teaching?" 971.

5. Kennedy, "How Does Professional Development Improve Teaching?" 946.

6. Mary Kennedy, "Parsing the Practice of Teaching," *Journal of Teacher Education* 67, no. 1 (2016): 10–13.

7. Malcolm Knowles, *The Modern Practice of Adult Education: From Pedagogy to Andragogy* (New York: Cambridge Books, 1980).

8. Sharan B. Merriam and Laura L. Bierema, *Adult Learning: Linking Theory and Practice* (San Fransisco: Jossey-Bass, 2013), 47.

9. Merriam and Bierema, *Adult Learning*, 47.

10. Forzani, "Understanding 'Core Practices' and 'Practice-Based' Teacher Education ," 357.

11. Pam Grossman, Sarah Schneider Kavanagh, and Christopher G. Pupik Dean, "The Turn Towards Practice in Teacher Education: An Introduction to the Work of the Core Practice Consortium," in *Teaching Core Practices in Teacher Education*, ed. Pam Grossman (Cambridge, MA: Harvard Education Press, 2021), 5.

12. See the TeachingWorks website at https://www.teachingworks.org/.

13. "High-Leverage Practices," webpage on the TeachingWorks website, https://www.teachingworks.org/work-of-teaching/high-leverage-practices.

14. Bradley Fogo, "Core Practices for Teaching History: The Results of a Delphi Panel Survey," *Theory & Research in Social Education* 42, no. 2 (2014): 176.

15. Fogo, "Understanding 'Core Practices' and 'Practice-Based' Teacher Education," 195.

16. Fogo, "Understanding 'Core Practices' and 'Practice-Based' Teacher Education," 177.

REFERENCES

Fogo, Bradley. "Core Practices for Teaching History: The Results of a Delphi Panel Survey." *Theory & Research in Social Education* 42, no. 2 (2014): 151–96. https://doi.org/10.1080/00933104.2014.902781.

Forzani, Francesca M. "Understanding 'Core Practices' and 'Practice-Based' Teacher Education: Learning from the Past." *Journal of Teacher Education* 65, no. 4 (2014): 357–68. https://doi.org/10.1177/0022487114533800.

Grossman, Pam, Sarah Schneider Kavanagh, and Christopher G. Pupik Dean. "The Turn Towards Practice in Teacher Education: An Introduction to the Work of the Core Practice Consortium." In *Teaching Core Practices in Teacher Education*, edited by Pam Grossman, 1–17. Cambridge, MA: Harvard Education Press, 2021.

Husbands, Chris, and Anna Pendry. "Continued Professional Development." In *History Teachers in the Making: Professional Learning*, edited by Anna Pendry, Chris Husbands, James Arthur, and Joe Davison, 121–45. Buckingham, UK: Open University Press, 1998.

Kennedy, Mary. "How Does Professional Development Improve Teaching?" *Review of Educational Research* 86, no. 4 (2016): 945–80. https://doi.org/10.3102/0034654315626800.

———. "Parsing the Practice of Teaching." *Journal of Teacher Education* 67, no. 1 (2016): 6–17. https://doi.org/10.1177/0022487115614617.

Knowles, Malcolm. *The Modern Practice of Adult Education: From Pedagogy to Andragogy.* New York: Cambridge Books, 1980.

Merriam, Sharan B., and Laura L. Bierema. *Adult Learning: Linking Theory and Practice.* San Francisco, CA: Jossey-Bass, 2013.

Opfer, V. Darleen, and David Pedder. "Conceptualizing Teacher Professional Learning." *Review of Educational Research* 81, no. 3 (2011): 376–407. https://doi.org/10.3102/0034654311413609.

Russ, Rosemary S., Bruce L. Sherin, and Miriam Gamoran Sherin. "What Constitutes Teacher Learning?" In *Handbook of Research on Teaching*, edited by Drew H. Gitomer and Courtney A. Bell, 391–438. Washington, DC: American Educational Research Association, 2016.

van Hover, Stephanie. "Professional Development of Social Studies Teachers." In *Handbook of Research in Social Studies*, edited by Linda S. Levstik and Cynthia A. Tyson, 352–72. New York: Routledge, 2008.

van Hover, Stephanie, and David Hicks. "History Teacher Preparation and Professional Development." In *International Handbook of History Teaching and Learning*, edited by Scott Alan Metzger and Lauren McArthur Harris, 391–418. Hoboken, NJ: Wiley-Blackwell, 2018.

1.5

A Teacher's Perspective

CherylAnne Amendola

CherylAnne Amendola teaches at Montclair Kimberly Academy in Montclair, New Jersey. As a passionate history educator, her participation in teacher professional development programs across the nation has bolstered her thinking and teaching.

One of my favorite stories to hook students in my class is about the time I was able to hold a lock of Thomas Jefferson's hair during a trip to the University of Virginia, which was coordinated by the Monticello Teacher's Institute. Most of the opportunities I've had, as an educator, to do deep soul-searching work as well as odd and fantastic activities have been through museum professional development programs. I've been able to draw students into history in ways I'd never been able to imagine. Additionally, as a lifelong learner myself, who feels the consistent need to enhance her craft by partnering with museum educators who understand the needs of teachers and the diversity of their experiences, I know that professional development has brought my content knowledge and pedagogy practices to an entirely new level. I've used museum resources and staff expertise to develop lessons and unit plans, and I've worked with staff to brainstorm ways to combine museum offerings with grade-level-appropriate pedagogy. I return to professional development with museums time and time again, because I've learned that not only do my students and I benefit from the time I spend at official programming, but also the continued relationship between the museum and participating educators and relationships forged between educators at museum programming have had an even greater, more lasting impact on me and my students. In this chapter, I will reflect on my experience learning new content and pedagogy skills at museums, hoping that you will get a better idea of what teachers need from museum staff when attending professional development programs.

Optimal museum programming is a dual-approach model in which teachers become students for part of the time and then have a chance to reflect and to develop ways to integrate what they have learned into their pedagogy. Having the opportunity to learn from experts through lectures, hands-on learning, and immersive experiences has allowed me and my colleagues to deepen our content knowledge. By deepening my content knowledge, I have been better able to marry the pedagogical sessions led by museum educators to the ideas I want my students to learn. For example, at the Monticello Teacher Institute, a teacher's "home base" is in a classroom, which puts forth a clear message that the program's goal is to deepen educators' knowledge before expecting them to be able to work with what they have learned to produce something tangible for their classrooms. Teachers spend a significant amount of time with museum staff learning about life at Monticello and are given several specialized tours of Jefferson's home and the grounds. From being able to conduct research in the Jefferson Library to meditating in Jefferson's Garden, Monticello's staff honored me as both an expert teacher and as a learner, and the fact that they took the time to strike that balance was invaluable.

One particularly powerful learning experience was the "Slavery at Monticello" tour. A museum researcher and expert guided us through the lives of enslaved people by taking us through Jefferson's home and pointing out evidence of enslaved black lives that were deeply intertwined with those of the white residents at Monticello. We were also brought through the gardens and other original and rebuilt structures on Mulberry Row so that we could see enslavement contextualized within each space. Monticello also offered teachers the experience of tasting food made from recipes and ingredients that were used by the Jefferson family and enslaved cooks like James Hemmings. Other museum staff, such as archaeologists, joined us in the classroom to bring artifacts to life and teach us how objects are used to interpret the past. Teachers are given access to the Jefferson Library and several hours of reading time to pursue passion projects that will turn into lesson plans.

It is an educator's dream to be surrounded by books in a beautiful space and given the gift of time to read about subjects on which they're passionate. I dug into Thomas Jefferson's *Farm Book*, so that I could find the names of those who, to me, had remained nameless because of their status as enslaved. I looked at Jefferson's drawings of inventions that he dreamed up. When Monticello took us to the special collections at the University of Virginia, we got to hold letters written by Jefferson and

Adams! The format of the Monticello Teacher Institute is designed to be a series of meaningful learning experiences for teachers. Optimal museum programming for educators allows teachers plenty of time and space for thinking and growing for the sake of learning, which helps those educators meet and exceed museum expectations for lesson design. Perhaps most importantly, museum experiences such as the one from Monticello make teachers feel valued. When I attended the Monticello Teacher Institute, I felt that they valued me as a teacher, learner, and human being. The Monticello Teacher Institute quenched my thirst for knowledge but also met my need to collaborate with educators with varying experiences, and it fed my soul. Museums have a sacred opportunity to enrich the lives of the educators they serve by designing programming that, by its nature, communicates to teachers that they are intelligent, valuable, and worthy of the time and effort it takes to organize such events.

Teachers can use museum resources and staff expertise to develop lessons and unit plans, brainstorming ways to combine museum offerings with grade-level-appropriate pedagogy. Museum educators must be well versed in teaching methods for the grade levels of the teachers they are serving. While not necessarily museum professional development, every experience I've had with professional development through the Gilder Lehrman Institute for American History has had both professional historians and master teachers as part of its teacher seminars. The historian focuses on content, and then the master teacher gives suggestions and helps teachers develop lesson and unit plans based on the content learned. For example, when one of the presenting historians used Paul Revere's engraving of the Boston Massacre at one of the seminars, the master teacher demonstrated how she uses that same engraving in the classroom as a way to help teachers learn methods of teaching image source analysis.

Museum staff need to be able to "think like teachers"—meaning, the programming they plan, and the artifacts they choose to present, need to be adaptable to lesson plans and accessible to students. Museum educators should be able to give ideas to teachers about how to use what they're presenting. In addition to having teachers create lesson plans based on the museum's holdings, it is also helpful for museum educators to present what they think would be good ways to put those holdings to use in the classroom. For example, if museum staff present teachers with the findings of an archaeological dig done on-site, it is necessary to help teachers develop ways to use those findings with their students to interpret the past. When I observed an archaeological dig at Monticello, one of the archaeologists found a button. While it was a seemingly insignificant object, this button told a story. By examining it thoroughly and seeing the pattern and design, as well as finding out the material from which it was made, I learned more about the community of enslaved people who were seemingly lost to time, because they didn't live in permanent structures and they were never centered in any historical story. From that button and other objects that turned up on the dig, I learned how and where these people stored their valuables and what they considered valuable, and I learned something about their living and eating patterns. I was taken aback by what could be learned from buttons and a couple of bones in the ground; that wonder stuck with me. It's that awe of discovery that I try to replicate for students in my classes, day after day, and I felt that awe very deeply at the archaeological site that day.

I was lucky enough to attend one of the Smithsonian American Art Museum's weeklong institutes. At the Smithsonian, museum educators not only take teachers on walks through their galleries but also hold frequent discussions about how the art can be integrated into their classrooms. Many ideas came from the museum itself, which then helped teachers develop their ideas. For example, before visiting the Smithsonian, I knew very little about Thomas Cole's Hudson River School paintings; however, with help from the guides, I was able to not only view several of Cole's works but also understand them within the context of American history. The staff also taught me how to look at and analyze art, which is a skill that I had not previously practiced. I was able to take that skill and bring it to my classroom, so my students would be able to see history in an entirely different way. Once I appreciated the way Cole's paintings captured the American landscape as unique, and was able to feel the American wilderness through his paintings, I had a new dimension in which to teach. It felt good to be able to develop and strengthen a different muscle and bring something into my teaching repertoire that I'd not considered before.

When planning teacher experiences, museum education coordinators should always keep in mind the diverse experiences of the educators who attend their programming, as they need to ensure their programming is accessible to everyone in attendance. Teachers need to be able to come away with usable lesson plans; the museum cannot offer resources for classroom use that require supplies to which the teacher has no access. Museum programs need to offer online, synchronous options for using museum resources as well as offer alternative offline content. The Smithsonian American Art Museum's teacher institute is a program that gives teachers a variety of ways to use museum content so that each teacher comes away from the institute with something they can use. During my attendance, museum educators offered print versions of lessons and art as well as print posters for use, in addition to their web-based services.

Furthermore, planning programming to ensure there is a cohort of educators with diverse backgrounds as well as including teachers from a variety of school types increases the impact of the program for attendees.

Throughout my teaching career, I have learned the most from teachers who not only teach in vastly different types of schools but also live a different life experience than I do. Being able to talk to one another about how we interpret the material presented by the museum's professional development staff, the way we would present what we've learned to our students, and our reasons for attendance deepens the experience of museum professional development programming. Bonding in teacher cohorts and with friendly, knowledgeable museum staff are two of the most integral parts of museum professional development learning experiences for educators. I have made friends and keep in touch with dozens of educators from museum programs that I have attended. Museum programs allow teachers to add people—both other teachers and museum staff—to their personal learning networks, upon which they can draw for years to come. I use social media to frequently speak and exchange ideas with the educators I've met during professional development, and I am regularly in touch with the staff from museum programs that I have attended. Even after the program has ended, together, we continue to wrestle with the material we learned as we design and refine ideas for lessons. Museum staff can help facilitate continued learning by leveraging email lists and social media to help keep participants engaged with one another. Current platforms such as Facebook groups are excellent ways to facilitate communication between participants. I've found and retained friendships I never could have had without the careful selection processes of the programs I've attended, which made sure there would be a wide range of people from different areas of the country and different types of schools.

In addition to opportunities to learn and create lesson plans in groups, recreational activities and ice breakers for educators attending museum professional development programs give value to the experience. Fostering attitudes of collegiality and sharing between teachers opens the door for greater and deeper participation in the program. Programs can encourage teachers to eat meals together, coordinate activities outside the program for them, and allow teachers to have more casual time to be together during programming. As a result, spaces become safer for teachers to take risks, make mistakes, and bounce ideas off of one another. For example, at the very beginning of the Monticello Teacher Institute, museum educators welcomed the teachers with hors d'oeuvres and mingling on one of the terraces. As teachers got to know one another, it became easier to have conversations about the difficult topics that naturally come up when talking about Jefferson and slavery. Teachers began to trust one another to have challenging conversations throughout the weeklong institute because they were given the opportunity to learn about one another personally, as well as professionally, through activities that were "just for fun." I've traveled to many places for the first time as a result of professional development programs. It's really fun to get to know and experience a new place with the people you're learning with!

Overall, I would describe my experiences with museum programming as not only positive but in many cases life-changing. The programs I've been lucky enough to attend have had museum educators at the helm who work hard to create full experiences for the teachers in attendance. Between the selection process that brings in teachers from many different walks of life and the division of time educators spend as learners and as teachers, I've been able to bring back new content and pedagogical methods to my classes over the years. Because I was able to grow both personally and professionally through each program I attended, I continue to participate in museum professional development opportunities, and I encourage my colleagues to do so as well. The combined hard work of museum educators and teachers who attend their programs then enriches the learning experiences of the thousands of students who will collectively benefit. My students have certainly benefitted from what I've learned, and the relationships I've formed, and will hopefully continue to do so!

2

✛

Translating Content into Pedagogical Content Knowledge

Christine Baron

Over the past thirty years, considerable effort has been aimed at encouraging "historical thinking" among teachers and students of history. Promoting historical thinking for teachers and students of history presupposes that the skills and practices of academic historians can be transposed into classroom practices. For museum educators working at historic sites, the idea of encouraging teachers to employ historical thinking skills and be more "historian like" seems a natural extension of the work of the sites into a practice that is transferable to the classroom.

However, across several studies, I and other researchers have shown stark differences in the ways in which teachers and historians encounter historic sites, the domains of knowledge upon which they draw, and the places where their expertise overlap. The picture emerging from the research is clear: teachers are no less experts than historians, they're expertise is just in an entirely different domain—namely, *teaching* history rather than researching and interpreting it. Appropriately, they draw upon the domain in which their expertise is situated to make sense of the historic space. Unlike recreational visitors, teachers who come to historic sites for professional development are self-selecting adult professionals attempting to solve a professional problem—to remediate and build their own knowledge/skills related to the particular content presented at the historic site for use in their classrooms. Teachers come to historic sites with expertise—known as *pedagogical content knowledge*—essential for solving that problem. Pedagogical content knowledge is the "special amalgam" of knowledge of students, content, and pedagogical knowledge along with the ability to combine these disparate elements for effective teaching.

In short, it appears that the primary difference between how historians and teachers attempt to solve the problem posed by the historic site is directionality: when presented with a historic site, historians delve deep in an attempt to understand the layers of meaning presented by the structures and material culture. Teachers, instead, take their understandings and almost immediately turn back to consider how to interpret what they encounter for their students.[1]

Over the years, I have found the metaphor of pelicans and pearl divers useful in explaining these differences. If one imagines the historic site as a body of water, then the historians act as pearl divers: diving ever deeper, making note of each layer they encounter, in their singular search for some undiscovered gem. Teachers encounter the site more like pelicans: diving into the first few layers of the water, retrieving some interesting morsel, and immediately navigating the complicated transition from swimming to flying to feed their young. Where historians search for the furthest bits of knowledge, lingering to grasp what is just out of reach, teachers glean information from the historic site and almost immediately begin to translate that into useful information for their students.

Understanding the essential purposes for which historians and teachers encounter historic places is critical for understanding how they view the resources available to them. Again, consider the pearl diver historians: the purpose of their visit is to find novel materials with which to construct new works—books, articles, and/or interpretive materials of some kind. For historians functioning in a world of publications and interpretive programs, the unexplored depths provide the greatest thrill and likelihood of success.

For the pelican teachers, everything they do, including historic site visits, serves a fundamentally different purpose: it is not to explore the new or novel but to educate students and create functioning members of society. The challenge that historic sites pose for teachers is about constructing a situation in which their students might successfully encounter the information from a historic site, it is about integrating it back into the classroom and into their lives beyond. They seek evocative experiences for their students that will inspire students' interest in the subject matter with which they are already engaged. For their students, teachers seek clarity about and inspiration from historical challenges, turmoil, or daily life in a particular age to illuminate the struggles of what it means to be a fully functioning person in the world.[2]

The misunderstanding this dichotomy presents for museum educators centers on the desire to provide teachers with the gems of the site and its collections. In the most basic sense, there is a desire to be good hosts for guests, especially for honored guests like teachers. Offering the very best of a site's collection to teachers is rooted in pride in the collection and respect for the work of teachers. However, neither pelicans nor children can survive on pearls alone, so we should cease to be surprised that teachers seem either uninterested in or refuse to pass along the "pearls" that historic sites offer. This is to neither state nor imply that teachers are not intellectually capable of engaging in these deep-dive expeditions into new materials; it is simply not the purpose of their visits. For people who spend their days engaged in the depths, that fundamental difference in the purpose of teachers' visits can be very quickly lost or misinterpreted.

What is necessary, then, is not to make historians think more like teachers or teachers think more like historians. Rather, we must understand how considerations of historic site materials diverge so we can create effective programming that addresses teachers' professional needs.

Teacher Thinking at Historic Sites

Even with intensive preparation in using historical methods, teachers do not interpret historic sites in ways consistent with the historical thinking practices of historians. Historians see historic places as texts to be read. For teachers, the historic site is a tool to consider using to convey lessons to their students.

Their students are the primary lens through which teachers view every aspect of the historic site. Through this lens, teachers filter their understanding of the substance of the site to ascertain what would be useful, helpful, or interesting to their students. They do not navigate the site alone but do so with their students—past and present, generally and specifically—with their innumerable strengths, weaknesses, needs, and interests. They connect the site experiences to the courses they teach, and relate to those experiences largely as they envision themselves with students, either at the site or in their own classrooms. While historians in these studies spoke of how "I"—they themselves—would use or understand, the teachers emphasized how "they"—their students—would use the site.[3]

For many teachers, content of the site is a remote secondary, or even tertiary, consideration. Teachers tend to focus on developing an accurate sense of the persons and events of the past, including clarifying prior "common" knowledge and "myth-busting" elements of history that they are responsible for teaching.[4] Focusing solely on presenting the content of the site and the pearls of the collection in historic site-based teacher professional development assumes a different set of goals and considerations than the ones teachers actually bring. In no way should this be regarded as dismissing the need for historical content to be part of teachers' professional development. Content is important. However, even content offered at historic sites that tells stories of individuals and events that are most central to American history curricula might equal a week's worth of lessons. Far more likely, it is allotted a day or two in an entire school year.

Focusing instead on historical concepts—the big ideas that thread throughout the school year—does far more to support teachers' ability to explain history to their students and increases the likelihood of them using the information gathered during historic site-based teacher professional development at multiple points throughout the year. In this way, teachers can focus on accurately grasping the conceptual significance of the stories in the microcosm of the site so they can help students comprehend the larger whole.[5]

Beyond that, teachers' considerations of historic sites tend to fall into pedagogically oriented categories:

- *Utility:* Teachers ask themselves how they could use the site in their classroom, identifying curricular connections, interesting perspectives, and opportunities for student engagement. Topics and materials without strong curricular connections are generally interesting to teachers as adult learners but offer little in the way of useful information for their classroom work.
  - *What this looks like:* At Monticello, teachers often get excited about Jefferson's Wheel Cypher, which is a cylinder with letters on stacked wheels used to encode and decode messages. However, with few curricular connections, unless teachers are planning curriculum units on spying, this device generates few lessons.
- *Logistics:* Teachers consider the logistics of maneuvering students through the physical space and social/behavioral expectations of the site. This extends to online platforms or handout materials and the ways in which they need to be adapted or transformed for students to use them successfully.
  - *What this looks like:* When walking into a historic space, teachers survey the room for how large it is relative to the size of the group they would bring. Is it an open space, like the battlefield at Antietam, requiring little physical restriction in terms of what can or cannot be touched, but also requiring students to gather together to hear site staff? Or is it more like the JFK Presidential Library, where the displays are interactive, move visitors in one direction, and all terminate in the same space? Here, depending on the age of the students, little direct instruction is needed, and they can move through the space more at their own pace, meeting up at the end.
- *Decoding:* Teachers raise questions about how well or how much students would be able to understand the site. The density of inter-

pretive text (decoding as literacy skill) as well as the complexity of the symbolic and historical text (decoding as historiography) of the site relative to contemporary understanding are part of the decoding work that teachers consider doing with or for their students.

- ∘ *What this looks like:*
  - Decoding as literacy skill frequently takes the form of providing alternate wording for comprehension. When a guide notes that a historical figure was "defenestrated," the teacher may interject, "They were thrown out a window."
  - As historiography, decoding might appear as a teacher explaining that, "No, in the 1880s, women did not suddenly grow excessively large buttocks, but bustles were very fashionable, and as weird as it may look to us, our fashions would look weird to people from that era."
- *Interpretation:* Teachers consider site materials with strong curricular connections, including or excluding topics that might be overly complex, are not age-/developmentally appropriate, would require considerable explanation, or are politically polarizing. They also consider the ways in which they would frame the history presented to show relationships, significance, or connections to the curriculum or narratives of the history they are trying to convey.
  - ∘ *What this looks like:* At the Old South Meeting House in Boston, there is a display of Margaret Sanger, an early advocate for women's reproductive rights. Nearly all the teachers in that study indicated they would not highlight this display, as it would raise issues with parents and community stakeholders that would outweigh or overshadow the purpose of the visit.

Supporting teachers as they work through these pedagogical orientations requires an understanding of and appreciation for the complexity of the professional problem-solving in which teachers are engaged. For museum educators, this means working with teachers to find out what they need, if possible, before they come on-site. It also means that even if there are teachers in an advisory group/role, it is important to recognize the limitations of the perspectives of teachers who know your site well. The "history nerds" we love to work with are invaluable resources for understanding a teacher's perspective, but they are rarely representative of the larger population. Each teacher brings with them the specific challenges of their classroom. Finding out what problems teachers are trying to address in their own classrooms is essential for enacting substantive, effective professional development.

There are so many means by which to help teachers translate a site's content into pedagogical content knowledge they can share with their students: hands-on activities, debriefing tours and lectures, and facilitated collaborations with their peers. Take a look at session ideas from TPD programs around the country at teacherinsites.org.

NOTES

1. Christine Baron, "Understanding Historical Thinking at Historic Sites," *Journal of Educational Psychology* 104, no. 3 (2012): 833–47; Christine Baron, "Using Inquiry-Based Instruction to Encourage Teachers' Historical Thinking at Historic Sites," *Teaching and Teacher Education* 35 (2013): 157–69; Christine Baron, Sherri Sklarwitz, Hyeyoung Bang, and Hanadi Shatara. "Understanding What Teachers Gain from Professional Development at Historic Sites," *Theory & Research in Social Education* 47, no. 1 (2019): 76–107.; Christine Baron, Sherri Sklarwitz, Hyeyoung Bang, and Hanadi Shatara, "What Teachers Retain from Historic Site-Based Professional Development," *Journal of Teacher Education* 71, no. 4 (2020): 392–408, https://doi.org/10.1177/0022487119841889; Christine Baron, Sherri Sklarwitz, and M. Blanco, "Assessment of Teachers' Gains Across Multiple Historic Site-Based Professional Development Programs," *Teaching and Teacher Education* 93 (2020): 103077.

2. Baron, "Using Inquiry-Based Instruction to Encourage Teachers' Historical Thinking at Historic Sites."

3. Baron, "Using Inquiry-Based Instruction to Encourage Teachers' Historical Thinking at Historic Sites."

4. Baron et al., "Understanding What Teachers Gain from Professional Development at Historic Sites."

5. Baron et al., "Understanding What Teachers Gain from Professional Development at Historic Sites"; Baron, Sklarwitz, Bang, and Shatara "What Teachers Retain from Historic Site-Based Professional Development."

REFERENCES

Baron, Christine. "Understanding Historical Thinking at Historic Sites." *Journal of Educational Psychology* 104, no. 3 (2012): 833–47.

———. "Using Inquiry-Based Instruction to Encourage Teachers' Historical Thinking at Historic Sites." *Teaching and Teacher Education* 35 (2013): 157–69.

Baron, Christine, Sherri Sklarwitz, Hyeyoung Bang, and Hanadi Shatara. "Understanding What Teachers Gain from Professional Development at Historic Sites." *Theory & Research in Social Education* 47, no.1, (2019): 76–107.

————. "What Teachers Retain from Historic Site-Based Professional Development." *Journal of Teacher Education* 71, no. 4 (2020): 392–408. https://doi.org/10.1177/0022487119841889.

Baron, Christine, Sherri Sklarwitz, and M. Blanco. "Assessment of Teachers' Gains Across Multiple Historic Site-Based Professional Development Programs." *Teaching and Teacher Education* 93 (2020): 103–77.

Chi, Michelene T. H. "Two Approaches to the Study of Experts' Characteristics." In *The Cambridge Handbook of Expertise and Expert Performance*, 21–30. New York: Cambridge University Press, 2006.

Hall, Timothy D., and Renay Scott. "Closing the Gap between Professors and Teachers: 'Uncoverage' as a Model of Professional Development for History Teachers." *The History Teacher* 40, no. 2 (2007): 257–63. doi:10.2307/30036992.

Shulman, Lee. "Knowledge and Teaching: Foundations of the New Reform." *Harvard Educational Review* (1986): 1–22.

Voss, James F. and J. Wiley. "Conceptual Understanding in History." *European Journal of Psychology of Education* 12 (1997): 147–58.

Voss, James, S. Tyler and L. Yengo. "Individual Differences in the Solving of Social Science Problems." In *Individual Differences in Cognition*, edited by R. F. Dillon & R. R. Schmeck. New York: Academic Press, 1983.

Voss, James, T. Greene, T. Post, and B. Penner. "Problem Solving in the Social Studies." In *Psychology of Learning and Motivation*, edited by H. Bower, 165–213. New York: Academic Press, 1983.

Wineburg, Samuel. "Reading Abraham Lincoln: An Expert/Expert Study in the Interpretation of Historical Texts." *Cognitive Science* 22, no. 3 (1998): 319–46.

Wineburg, Samuel S. "Historical Problem Solving: A Study of the Cognitive Processes Used in the Evaluation of Documentary and Pictorial Evidence." *Journal of Educational Psychology* 83, no. 1 (1991): 73–87.

3

Antiracism

The Both/And to Shaping Change

Dina A. Bailey

Both/And. It is the concept that multiple ideas can be true at the same time. For example, the United States is a land of opportunity, *and* there is not equal opportunity in the US. The United States has been built on the concept that "all men are created equal," *and* people have never been treated equally in the US. Race is a social construct originally created by individuals (meaning it is learned rather than biological), *and* racism is so interwoven with social systems and hierarchies that it no longer needs individual actors to sustain it. How do teachers work to center this understanding that multiple ideas can be true at the same time? When (if ever) should this concept *not* be centered during the educational development of critical thinkers? Candidly, how/why/when should teachers recognize the intersectionality of human experiences while also recognizing the importance of practicing authentic equity? Intersectionality and equity are not mutually exclusive.

This chapter is meant to provide a context and framework for later chapters that discuss, in detail, more specific examples of teacher professional development. Central to this chapter is a discussion of race, racism, and antiracism in an effort to encourage reflections on racial inequity—and what responsibility teachers have—as the book progresses. Further scholarship can be found by authors such as Michelle Alexander, Carol Anderson, Eduardo Bonilla-Silva, Kimberlé Crenshaw, Robin DiAngelo, Joe R. Feagin, Crystal M. Fleming, Tanya Maria Golash-Boza, Ijeoma Oluo, Layla F. Saad, Bryan Stevenson, and Ibram X. Kendi (to name a few). At this point, there is such a gap in racial experience and viewpoints that racism can be largely invisible to some *and* hyper-visible to others.

Over the past few years, the rise of voices of color, paired with more research into systemic discrimination and the widespread dissemination of video proof of injustices against people of color, especially black people, has brought both a wave of urgency and a rise in collective consciousness when it comes to racism in the United States. Some teachers have been encouraged to review their curricula and more directly utilize critical race theory. Others have literally been banned from teaching anything perceived as having to do with it. As with other fields, polarization within the education sphere has intensified over the past decade. The scrutiny has led to higher anxiety, tension, and frustration—and, ultimately, the teacher "shortage" has become a teacher "crisis" as growing numbers of individuals move into other fields where their skills are transferrable.

For those who have stayed in the classroom, calls have become louder for methodological/content support from academic scholars and other educational experts. Additionally, teachers have asked for safe spaces to share what is going on in their classrooms and within their districts. Brave spaces are also being created where teachers can experiment and critically reflect before proposing initiatives/learning units to their peers and department heads. The country is ripe for systemic change in the educational realm. Museums and historic sites have the opportunity and responsibility to expand their professional development offerings to be of greatest service to teachers through meeting these needs.

However, before we can hope to change these systems, there must first be a shared understanding of the fundamental definition of racism. While racism can be understood to be global at this point, it does show up differently, depending on a country's geographic and social history (and present). The definition discussion for this chapter should be viewed through a United States lens and appropriately applied to case studies in the chapters to come.

One of the most common definitions of racism is simply that it includes any prejudice against someone because of their race. The other common definition is that racism is a system of advantage, based on race, that benefits white people and disadvantages people of color, with the understanding that in order for racism to take place, it requires both prejudice and power. While the definitions are similar in many ways, the differences drastically change how people understand and work to address racism in the US. When we use the first definition, we inaccurately reduce racism to individuals and the need to change only individual minds and feelings. When we use the second definition, we acknowledge the systems of power that prompt and reinforce racist behaviors and racist ideas. It is the system—and our complacency and intentional/unintentional complicity within it—that gives racism its power. With more than four hundred years of systemic racial oppression, generations of people have struggled under a distinct power disadvantage that negates the possibility of actually having a level (equal) playing field for individuals or for collectives. How we define racism also helps us determine how to abolish it and the urgency with which we combat it. In recognizing racism as a systemic problem, we can act in ways that have larger impacts that ripple farther out. Racism, as well as other oppressive-isms, can be traced from the very creation of US education. It can be heard in debates about types of school systems (public, private, charter, etc.). It can be felt in the canons utilized and the historical/contemporary figures who are amplified as well as those whose contributions are ignored. It can be seen in classrooms that are just as segregated today, if not more so, than they were at the beginning of the US civil rights movement. Racism has infiltrated the system(s) that supports education in the US—both in formal and informal ways.

The Both/And to Why It's So Hard

We can intellectually recognize the truths of racism, *and* they can still make us feel angry, frustrated, scared, and uncertain. We can recognize that blackness and whiteness are constructed *and* shy away from how we experience advantages or disadvantages, successes or losses, based on those constructions. We can know that racism is not just about black people and white people; yet, we so often reduce it to these two racial group memberships—which continues to make the struggles of other racial group identities more invisible. As many antiracists have written about extensively, for some the smallest amount of racial stress can become intolerable and trigger a desire to divert. For others, racial stress occurs so often that it has become part of those individuals' everyday experiences. Because of all this, we have learned how to use what Joan Olsson calls "detours":

- I'm colorblind
- the rugged individual and the bootstrap theory
- reverse racism
- blame the victim
- innocent by association
- the white knight or white missionary
- the white wash
- I was an Indian in a former life
- the isolationist
- bending over backward
- BWAME (but what about me)
- teach me, please
- white on white, and righteously so

- the certificate of innocence
- smoke and mirrors
- the accountant
- silence
- exhaustion and despair[1]

These detours often close further exploration before a nuanced conversation can even really begin. Here, power and privilege are made visible through the ability to effectively end an experience, which stymies individual and collective growth. Part of the desire to curtail such experiences lies in a heretofore dominant paradigm that envisions racist words and/or actions as discrete, individual, intentional, and malicious. This is the good/bad binary where good people can't be racist and only bad people are racist. There are a lot of people who act in blatant and unapologetically racist ways; however, from both an individual and a societal viewpoint, racism is often much more subtle/implicit. Individuals have been nurtured by an increasingly quieter, though no less violent, version of the same oppressive system that has been insidiously interwoven into the fabric of our society. It is the system—and our complacency within the system—rather than "simply" individual intent that gives racism its power. Systemic racism is a machine that continuously runs, no longer needing individual actors to pull the levers; by just letting it be (not actively dismantling the machine), we each hold responsibility for what the machine continues to produce.

As teachers are thinking about the racial equity work that they can support within their classrooms, and as there are increased expectations around the centering of racial equity in professional development settings, "detour-spotting" can be critical to individual and collective progress. We must become more aware of when we, and others, divert; we must name it when it happens; and we must empathetically "call in" (rather than "call out") ourselves and others in order to make progress. This growth in awareness should be paired with a growth in knowledge/understanding.

In order to grow, we must embrace a more complex understanding of racism because how we define racism also determines how we fight against it. As Ibram X. Kendi writes in *How to Be an Antiracist*,

> A racist is someone who is supporting a racist policy by their actions or inaction or expresses a racist idea. An antiracist is someone who is supporting an antiracist policy by their actions or expressing an antiracist idea. "Racist" and "antiracist" are like people name tags that are placed and replaced based on what someone is doing or not doing, supporting or expressing in each moment.[2]

He urges individuals not to see these identifiers as permanent tattoos but, rather, as working toward one end of the spectrum or the other: "We can only strive to be one or the other. We can unknowingly strive to be a racist. We can knowingly strive to be an antiracist. Like fighting an addiction, being an antiracist requires persistent self-awareness, constant self-criticism, and regular self-examination."[3] In this paradigm, racist and antiracist are not fixed identities; we can be an antiracist in one moment but be a racist in another, based on the decisions we make. Each action becomes a barometer of what we are instead of a fixed value judgment identifying who we are. Teacher professional development trainings, and practical application within the classroom, can emphasize the fluid nature of this spectrum while emphasizing personal agency and responsibility within the context of power and privilege. This is one space where an intersectional framework can be critical to individual and collective progress.

Intersectionality and the Both/And of Being an Antiracist

Kimberlé Crenshaw developed intersectionality as a theoretical framework that utilizes both/and. Essentially, returning to the concept of identities, intersectionality recognizes that our complicated identities (race, ethnicity, gender, sexual orientation, socioeconomic status, etc.) cannot be discussed in isolation from each other. It is not about listing one's identities as fixed aspects of being in an aim to acknowledge diversity; intersectionality is "a necessary analytic tool to explain the complexities and realities of discrimination and of power or the lack thereof, and how they intersect with identities . . . multiple oppressions reinforce each other to create new categories of suffering."[4] It is a way in which we can see ourselves and each other with more complexity, and at the same time, it can be used as a framework for larger social change efforts that challenge complex systems of discrimination and oppression.

Many people are well-intentioned; they want to consistently make antiracist decisions and take antiracist actions—to remain on that side of Kendi's spectrum. They are consciously committed to a world that abolishes racism. They are determined to grow through cross-racial experiences. And they intellectually believe in concepts like equity and inclusion. And sometimes our stated/conscious values are not in alignment with our implicit biases and prejudices. So, in very practical ways, as teachers and those who facilitate teacher professional development, how do we become change agents for ourselves and for others?

First, we must become aware of the power of socialization, which often creates and reinforces oppressive systems. As DiAngelo notes, "whereas our personal narratives vary, we are all swimming in the same racial water."[5] Or to use another visual, we are all breathing in the same pollution and being mentally, physically, and emotionally affected by it. Kendi often describes racism as a metastatic cancer that has spread to nearly every part of the human (individual) body and (collective) experience. Institutionally racist policies have infiltrated all aspects of our lives and support the persistence of stereotypes, biases, and prejudices that lead to individual discrimination and collective oppression. Powerful people have developed racist policies through self-interest; these policies, then, promote racist ideas to justify the inequitable effects of the policies; and those ideas continue to spark ignorance and hate in a cycle that has yet to end. Becoming aware of the systems and patterns of our lives (and educational systems), impacts how we intentionally and unintentionally have become complicit in and/or enablers of racist systems; this is essential to changing how we experience and participate in the world. That said, "[U]nderstanding how racism works and how White privilege functions within our society does not bring us any closer to justice."[6] Becoming more aware through a knowledge of these truths is only the first move.

Second is a deep understanding of intersectionality as both a way to understand our individual, unique experiences and our collective, shared experiences of privilege and oppression. It is a both/and that everyone is different based on the unique combination of their identities and experiences, *and* everyone is valuable through the understanding of our similarities and differences. In her book, *So You Want to Talk About Race*, Ijeoma Oluo voices her belief that "Tying racism to its systemic causes and effects will help others see the important difference between systemic racism, and anti-white bigotry . . . the more practice you have at tying individual racism to the system that gives it power, the more you will be able to see all the ways in which you can make a difference."[7] Additionally, it is important to acknowledge that the pacing and pathways of change are multitudinous, iterative, and nonlinear. Don't disparage or judge someone else's journey because it seems different from the path along which you move. Support and encourage others' movement in positive ways while focusing on the work that you need to do (i.e., the "glass houses" proverb). And internalize that intention and impact are not the same. We may intend one thing, and the impact can be very different. Great harm is often committed by people who are well-intentioned; when this happens—and it will—sincerely apologize and then actually do better. Within professional development trainings and our classrooms, consciously practicing how we separate intention from impact can increase empathy, resilience, and (genuine) accountability.

Third, be someone who uses "call in" rather than "call out" methodologies within the practice of antiracism. We often perpetuate harm under the guise of accountability. We often learn just enough to be dangerous before we start acting on the little we have learned. While the stated intention may be to hold people in their integrity, the impact can be virtue signaling.[8] adrienne maree brown has provided the following acknowledgments to provide clarity on calling people in rather than calling people out:

- You have the right to tell your own story; you do not have to be silent.
- You do not have the right to traumatize abusive people.
- You do have the right to walk away, to literally and virtually gather yourself up and remove yourself from the dynamic.
- You have the right to create boundaries that generate more possibilities for you.
- You have the right to ask for support from your friends/community.
- You are not obligated to engage in a process with someone.
- You have the right to not know the right moves to make in the moment.[9]

Fourth, build your antiracist educational practice on the idea of abolitionist teaching. This way of teaching is "built on the radical imagination of collective memories of resistance, trauma, survival, love, joy, and cultural modes of expression and practice that push and expand the fundamental ideas of democracy."[10] Being an abolitionist means that you are ready to lose something, that you are putting something on the line in order for there to be justice. In her book, Love reaches new heights with her ideas of abolitionist teaching by standing on the shoulders of Ella Baker, a prolifically courageous thinker and political organizer who was active before, during, and far after the period that we align with the US civil rights movement of the 1950s and 1960s. In building on Baker's dynamism, Love describes abolitionist teaching as being "built on the cultural wealth of students' communities and creating classrooms in parallel with those communities aimed at facilitating interactions where people matter to each other, fight together in the pursuit of creating a homeplace that represents their hopes and dreams, and resist oppression all while building a new future."[11] Creating an environment where abolitionist teaching is a framework that overlays all content curricula could be life-changing for all learners—regardless of their racial group identity(ies).

And, finally, create opportunities to practice individual and collective resilience. Generally, resilience is the ability to become strong, healthy, or successful again after something bad happens. We all fall in different ways and because of different obstacles in our paths. The practice of taking a quick moment to recognize why we fell, so that we know how to change future behaviors, and then the effort of rising again are essential to the idea of resilience. Added to that are the courage and vulnerability to put ourselves in positions where we might fall in the first place. We are not able to control all the events that happen to us in our lives, but we can decide to not be reduced by them. We can refuse to limit ourselves to the idea that we must "just" survive racist experiences. In her book, *Rising Strong: How the Ability to Reset Transforms the Way We Live, Love, Parent and Lead*, Brené Brown wrote a "Manifesto of the Brave and Brokenhearted." In part, the manifesto says, "There is no greater threat to the critics and cynics and fearmongers than those of us who are willing to fall because we have learned how to rise. With skinned knees and bruised hearts; we choose owning our stories of struggle, over hiding, over hustling, over pretending. When we deny our stories, they define us. When we run from struggle, we are never free."[12] But when we heal, we have more future capacity to heal ourselves and others. adrienne maree brown has discovered that "the work of cultivating personal resilience, healing from trauma, self-development, and transformation is actually a crucial way to expand what any collective body can be. We heal ourselves, and we heal in relationship, and from that place, simultaneously, we create more space for healed communities, healed movements, healed worlds."[13] As museum and classroom educators practice what resilience looks like, feels like, sounds like, and acts like, they can better support the learning / practicing of others. When we know better, we can do better, and we can teach better.

The Both/And of Showing Up in Our Power

There are moments when we have control, moments when we have influence, and moments when we are particularly invested in a process or an outcome. These are not either / or instances; they may all occur within the same moment. It is a recognition that sometimes within a given situation we have more passion than influence or more influence than control. This is not a divestment of responsibility—rather, it is inspiration to find and utilize agency with more nuance. It is an acknowledgment that there are some spaces where we have more power or advantage and some where we have less; this is true for everyone. It is an encouragement to center mutual transformation and find relationships through which you can evolve in your practice of antiracism. It is a reminder that we are each on a journey and that this work takes time—so we should conscientiously set aside time for the work *and* interweave the work through all aspects of our lives. It is a call to ground yourself in trust, starting with the mantra, "I trust myself in the face of the unknown." It is a rallying to align your beliefs, values, and actions—not just in the big moments but in the everyday interactions. As we move through the rest of the chapters in this book, considering where we are on our journey and what work we need to do—and what support we need—to move forward, here is one last thought from Desiree Evans:

> In building our movements, we learn this: we come from different places across the country and the world, we face different obstacles, paths, twists, and turns—some of us reshaping the very rocks beneath us, some of us moving the rocks with our combined strength, and some of us going around them when they can't be moved and finding another path to our desired goal. I've learned that those of us with the same dreams can find each other, and in finding each other, we can learn to move together, to build together, to shape the world together, to flow together, and maybe, just maybe . . . together we can reach the sea.[14]

May the ripples of your future antiracist actions combine into an overwhelming tidal wave that reaches a sea of change for our current and future learners.

NOTES

1. Joan Olsson, "Detour-Spotting for White Anti-Racists," *Racial Equity Tools,* 2011. https://www.racialequitytools.org/home.

2. Ibram X. Kendi, *How to Be an Antiracist* (New York: One World, 2019), 22–23.

3. Kendi, *How to Be an Antiracist.*

4. Bettina L. Love *We Want to Do More Than Survive: Abolitionist Teaching and the Pursuit of Educational Freedom* (Boston: Beacon Press, 2019), 3.

5. Robin J. DiAngelo, *White Fragility: Why It's So Hard for White People to Talk About Racism* (Boston: Beacon Press, 2018), 2.

6. Love,. *We Want to Do More Than Survive,* 51.

7. Ijeoma Oluo, *So You Want to Talk About Race* (New York: Seal Press, 2019), 35.

8. Virtue signaling is the action or practice of publicly expressing opinions or sentiments intended to demonstrate one's good character or the moral correctness of one's position on a particular issue.

9. adrienne maree brown, *Emergent Strategy: Shaping Change, Changing Worlds* (Chico: AK Press, 2017), 140–41.

10. Love, *We Want to Do More Than Survive,* 100.

11. Love, *We Want to Do More Than Survive,* 68.

12. Brené Brown. *Rising Strong: How the Ability to Reset Transforms the Way We Live, Love, Parent and Lead* (New York, Random House, 2017), 267.

13. brown, *Emergent Strategy,* 192.

14. Love, *We Want to Do More Than Survive,* 269–70.

3.5

A Teacher's Perspective

Alysha Butler-Arnold

Alysha Butler-Arnold teaches at McKinley Technology High School in Washington, DC. Here she shares how participating in place-based teacher professional development prompted her to engage students with their local history and community.

More than 90 percent of America's cemeteries were segregated on some level until the 1950s. Civil rights legislations failed to prevent their segregation because cemeteries were not considered public accommodations. It was not until the Supreme Court ruling under *Shelley v. Kraemer* that racial restrictions in land deeds were considered in violation of the Fourteenth Amendment and were declared unconstitutional. Prior to the ruling, black communities established their own cemeteries. To be able to still provide loved ones with a respectable resting place was in many ways a show of resistance. The demographics of many of these communities have since changed, and community leaders, through no fault of their own, have struggled to maintain the cemeteries.

Washington, DC, is a treasure trove for teachers in search of rich and fulfilling summer teacher professional development. In 2017, I enrolled in a two-week summer seminar with Ford's Theatre. I credit this one seminar with almost completely revolutionizing my entire teaching style and outlook. Showing educators how to teach history through monuments and sites was central to Ford's Theatre's mission, and their local field trips ignited an excitement within me that I had not felt since I was a little girl. My parents, grandparents, and great-grandparents gave me the keys to unlock the untold histories of my surroundings with their stories. But before that seminar, I had never thought of incorporating that same strategy in my classroom. On one trip, we briefly stopped at Mount Zion and Female Union Band Cemetery. The cemetery was established in 1808. The land was purchased by Ebenezer Eliason for $500 for the Montgomery Methodist Church as a resting place for both its white and black members. Eventually, black members of the church branched out and established their own church, called the Mount Zion United Methodist Church, albeit under the supervision of Montgomery Methodist Church. In 1842, the Female Union Band Society, a Free Black and Native American benevolent society, purchased neighboring land on the western border of the cemetery and, in the absence of a visible border, the cemetery began to be referred to collectively as Mount Zion Cemetery. Not only was the cemetery a burial ground for free and enslaved blacks, but it is believed that it was also used as a stop along the Underground Railroad. In 1849, Oak Hill Cemetery was created nearby, and soon whites stopped burying their loved ones in Mount Zion Cemetery and prohibited blacks from burying theirs in Oak Hill. White bodies buried in Mount Zion Cemetery were eventually disinterred and buried in Oak Hill while the black bodies were left in place. In 1879, Montgomery Methodist Church leased the cemetery to Mount Zion for burial rights with the agreement to maintain the site and erect a fence to separate Oak Hill from Mount Zion Cemetery. Although Oak Hill Cemetery was our main destination, we briefly stopped at Mount Zion and learned about its history. I could not believe that I was standing not only in the oldest black cemetery in the District, but in a place where some enslaved men, women, and children were finally able to find rest and where others hid with hopes of finding their freedom. Yet I felt saddened at the cemetery's dilapidated state. Some of the tombstones were broken, the grass was overgrown, and, believe it or not, some of the Georgetown residents were allowing their dogs to relieve themselves at the site. Before we moved next door to Oak Hill Cemetery, I took a few moments to wander off and view some of the messages on the tombstones. Along the way, I came across one that looked as if it was in the battle of its life against the weeds and vines that were threatening to completely overtake it. A plastic child's toy had been laid at the bottom of the headstone with such care that I just knew the gesture was deliberate, and the toy was not simply someone's displaced trash or litter. I had brought it to the attention of my tour guide, who said that such an occurrence was not uncommon and that other graves have had trinkets or toys placed next to them. I was touched by this act, for a variety of reasons. First, the cemetery is in a posh section of Georgetown. If you are not looking carefully, you can pass it or consider it inconsequential on your way to the more renowned Oak Hill Cemetery. In addition, because it was first established in 1808, I doubted any of the residents had living relatives remaining in the area. Lastly, burials at the cemetery ceased by the 1950s following its inability to meet certain city health codes.[1] Mount Zion Cemetery had all the ingredients to become a forgotten part of DC's history. Yet, the fact that someone had been visiting the cemetery on a regular basis to make this donation informed me that the black residents of the District had not forgotten it. As a District of Columbia Public School teacher, I am entrusted with the care of the children of the men and women of the District. My role extends beyond simply preparing my students for college; it includes helping to preserve and pass along the history of their community, whose demographics are drastically changing. If someone in the community cared enough to leave offerings to the cemetery's residents, the District's educators should at minimum pass along the story of the cemetery their ancestors worked so hard to maintain. When we arrived at Oak Hill Cemetery, the glaring contrast convinced me that something had to be done. The layout of the cemetery reminded me more of the inviting configuration of an old money country club than of a cemetery. None of the ailments that plagued Mount Zion Cemetery were present in Oak Hill Cemetery. I walked away knowing that I had to do something, but not believing that there was anything I could do. The belief that such racial inequity was the norm and could not be altered almost prevailed.

At the end of the year, DCPS students have one week of school remaining after their final exams. My school has always tried to create enriching activities for students during this week. In 2019, I remembered the cemetery and thought it would be worth a try to somehow get the students involved. I knew that the decay of the cemetery was too extensive to be corrected by the efforts of my students alone; however, I was more concerned with taking the students to the site and giving them an opportunity to show their reverence for the people who were buried there. My first step was finding a colleague to collaborate and brainstorm with. Such an endeavor had never been attempted by my school or District, and I needed someone who would support and encourage me and who was solution oriented. I solicited the help of my school's instructional coach, Carey Bednarz, who has an exceptional talent for making her fellow teachers feel that they can achieve any goal with proper planning. After we contacted the cemetery and received the green light to donate our time, we both focused on defining specific goals. What did we want our students to do at the cemetery? With what type of experience did we want our students to walk away from this activity? How would I relay the idea that this experience was meant to be not only a simple volunteer project but also an act of reverence and outward display of devotion for their ancestral community? My students may not have been able to restore the broken tombstones, but we could at least remove the weeds, vines, and litter that were threatening to overtake them. I also knew that I wanted to donate something from the school to the cemetery that would be there to remember this exceptional class, and we decided on a beautiful park bench with an engraved plaque, where visitors could sit and reflect. Finally, I wanted our students to participate in a humble dedication ceremony at which we would ask the residents of the cemetery to accept our gift and our day of service and make a promise to never forget those who were buried there.

The greatest obstacle that stood in our way was securing the necessary funds to finance the trip. A colleague had told me about GrantEd, which is a grant program to pay for education-related expenses up to $500. I was a little intimidated because I had never applied for a grant before; however, the process was simple, and I was elated when I discovered that I had been awarded a grant to pay for the field trip. My department chair, Lashunda Reynolds, was able to exhaust the last of our department money to cover transportation, and a fellow colleague's father-in-law whose family had a history of participating in the civil rights movement of the 1950s graciously donated money to feed the student volunteers.

I introduced the cemetery through a one-day lesson about its history to help my students become impassioned enough to care about its current and eventual fate, referring to the individuals buried there as "members of our community." I felt this terminology would appeal to all my students regardless of their racial background or whether they were a fifth-generation native born Washingtonian or recent immigrant from another state or country. I also did not want the lesson to be driven solely by the outrage of the glaring inequities between Mount Zion and Oak Hill Cemetery. I firmly believe that, as teachers, if we begin and end our lesson with discussions that simply focus on the obstacles, we leave no space for our students to explore their potential role as future problem solvers.

The day of the field trip, the original tour guide from Ford's Theatre who initially introduced me to the cemetery joined the students and me, as well as a local news crew. Before we began our cleanup, the students marched in line in a procession to a beautiful oak tree where select students volunteered to lead the group through a libation ceremony—in which liquid is poured out as an offering—to recognize all the individuals who were buried there. We then went to work clearing the weeds and trash. I had never seen my students so alive outside of the school building. Instead of hearing complaints from the students about working outside in the elements, I heard conversations about the tombstones, how happy they were to be outside, how they had never worked with plants, what it must have been like to hide in the cemetery while fleeing along the Underground Railroad, and how they hoped we could do this again next year. During our break for lunch, the students sat for a Q&A with Vernon Ricks, one of the first black students to integrate McKinley

Technology High School, who just so happened to also be a member of the cemetery board. Later, so many of the students would tell me that this was their favorite part of the field trip and they felt fortunate and privileged to meet an alumnus whose efforts enabled them to attend their school. After lunch, the students assembled for the park bench donation ceremony. Two students were selected to read a speech in which they promised to never forget the people who were buried at the cemetery and to continue to keep their story and legacy alive. After the speech, the students presented the park bench, which had been assembled by an all-girl STEM student volunteer group, to Mr. Ricks. Then each student, before boarding the bus to return home, recorded a two-minute exit interview in which they reflected on what participating in the project meant to them and whether history classes need to incorporate more civic-based projects like the cemetery project and why.

I had no idea how much our project would resonate within the community. One week after, I got a call from staff at a local radio station who saw our story on the local news and asked us if we could be guests on their station to receive a community award in recognition of our efforts to help clean up the cemetery. In addition, I was contacted by several McKinley Tech alumni asking if they could be involved in future volunteer projects at the cemetery. It even inspired teachers within my own school; that summer, we organized a "McKinley Day of Service," when incoming freshmen volunteered with local charities in the city. Looking back, I realize this project was possible for a variety of reasons: (1) I had access to quality teacher seminars, which helped me better understand the history of my community and took me to sites where I could hear the stories of the unheard and marginalized members of my community; (2) I had a teaching schedule that permitted exploration of creative, meaningful, and civic-based activities and time to collaborate and plan with other teachers; (3) I was given information about grants that could help fund my project; and (4) the most important component in the success of the project was my ability to solicit the assistance of my students. The students showed up because I introduced them to a historical site in their own neighborhood that held the history of their ancestors who needed their help. History was not dead, and I showed my students how they could keep it alive.

NOTE

1. National Park Service US Department of the Interior, "Historic American Landscapes Survey," 2008, http://lcweb2.loc.gov/master/pnp/habshaer/dc/dc1000/dc1064/data/dc1064data.pdf (accessed June 10, 2021).

4

✚

Interdisciplinary Connections

Learning about STEM at a History Museum

Kristen D. Burton and Robert Wallace

The typical, and valuable, professional development teachers receive at historical sites and museums centers on teaching history, or some other aspect of social studies, with content aligned to the nature of the site or museum. Museums and historical sites can also provide powerful interdisciplinary professional development experiences to teachers of other disciplines, in addition to history, by using the stories, events, and people they commemorate and document to cultivate learning experiences. The Real World Science Summer Teacher Seminar at the National World War II Museum in New Orleans, Louisiana, is designed to do just that.

The Real World Science program is a model that could extend to historical and place-based museums everywhere. Each historic house with a kitchen or a large garden, and each institution with a collection containing artifacts documenting how people once lived and worked, has the potential to connect those resources to stories that can engage students in both social studies and the sciences to learn about problem-solving in the past. Those learning experiences could be passed on through workshops and experiences that immerse participating teachers in the time period, along with pedagogical best practices for science education. What follows is a case study of what we learned from the evaluations and the experience of running a science, technology, engineering, and mathematics (STEM)-focused interdisciplinary program.

The Real World Science Program at the
National World War II Museum

The National World War II Museum offers professional development for teachers who teach science and STEM to fifth through eighth graders. Through the museum's Real World Science curriculum, we use the people, events, and stories of WWII to initiate science investigations around concepts students need to learn in upper elementary and middle school. The Real World Science Summer Teacher Seminar is a weeklong, on-site, intensive experience. This program trains the participating teachers to implement the Real World Science curriculum, along with best practices in science education. Part of the museum's mission is to highlight the significance of teaching the history of how WWII was fought, how the Allies won, and what the war means today. Curriculum and professional development programs at the museum look to connect the way people of the past approached and worked to solve the massive issues and conflicts of their time in order to help inspire possible solutions for large-scale problems people face today.

Teaching STEM at history sites has both challenges and advantages. It is not what most audiences expect, and it is not in everyone's area of expertise. Sometimes there is a concern that audiences will reject STEM activities or programs, perceiving them as out of context; but our surveys suggest that our audience feels the stories we tell about STEM and WWII support their understanding of the history of the era. Teaching STEM at a history site can be a challenge for museum educators as well, but we mitigate this hesitation by expecting that all the STEM we talk about at the museum ties directly to artifacts and oral histories we have in our collection. We may have a lesson that is more broadly related to WWII, such as Victory Gardens, but primarily tie our lessons and activities directly to objects from our collection. For example, we talk about the forces of flight, showing our seven airplanes on display with their different configurations of wing and fuselage sizes and shapes, and engine types and numbers. Or we talk about trajectory, with a discussion of how Norden bombsights worked in the background. While this requires both our educators and the teachers we train to understand STEM, as well as history, it pays off with deeper engagement and understanding of both subject areas.

The Real World Science program includes comprehensive evaluation that specifically examines the ways the museum served as a site of learning during the seminar, and how that place-based learning influenced the quality of the development experience. Teachers place great value on the pedagogical tools they learn and the curriculum they receive, but they often report that without the experience of being on-site at the museum, the seminar would not be as effective. We applied changes to the program based on these evaluations, conducted by the Science Museum of Minnesota, to increase the impact of the experience on teachers and the benefit to their students in turn. In particular, we focused on increasing access to the experience for teachers from Title 1 schools, both urban and rural, and thus extended our reach to underserved schools and their students. We aim to: (1) provide teachers with quality curricular activities they can use to engage students in authentic STEM learning experiences; (2) provide teachers with appropriate pedagogical tools to promote student thinking and reasoning with said activities; and (3) increase teachers' skills to integrate STEM subjects with history and literacy to make lessons more engaging and transformative.

The Cohort

By design, the Real World Science Summer Teacher Seminar welcomes a diverse cohort of teachers. Our grant from the Northrop Grumman Foundation stipulates that the teachers must teach science to students in fifth to eighth grades in a public school. This includes teachers who teach all subjects in a self-contained classroom, teachers who teach more than one subject (often science and social studies), and teachers who specialize in science. We emphasize in recruitment materials and application questions that we are looking for teachers who are relatively early in their careers and interested in being reflective on their practices. In reviewing applications, we focus on teachers with four to ten years of experience, including a few more experienced teachers who show a desire to continually improve their teaching, a passion for improving the lives of students, and the foundations of a teacher-leader. We balance the cohort to ensure that roughly half the teachers are from Title 1 schools and then seek an approximately even number of teachers from urban, suburban, and rural schools.

Recruitment

One challenge to an interdisciplinary program is recruiting applications. It is more challenging to get applications for this workshop than for our seminars aimed at social studies teachers. We advertise with the National Science Teaching Association and through associated state teacher organizations. Often, though, membership in these disciplinary organizations is lower for less-experienced teachers and for teachers in elementary and middle schools. These teachers sometimes think of themselves as elementary or middle school teachers first, and don't strongly identify as specialists. We have found that teachers in our target pool respond better to being referred by a colleague or supervisor, and most of our applicants have been encouraged to apply by such individuals. Part of our recruitment strategy is to have past cohort members run a short workshop in their own city or state after their weeklong experience. This fulfills our aim of developing teacher-leaders and helps spread the word about the program teacher-to-teacher. Between these teacher-run workshops and the short workshops run by our staff at conferences and other institutions, we make inroads with teachers, supervisors, and coaches. We also make the curricular activities freely available. Those who encounter the activities and see how they match STEM standards with history and literacy can see the power of tying this learning to specific artifacts and stories from WWII. Even if they don't want to attend the workshop, they are enthusiastic about using the curriculum and telling colleagues about both it and the workshop.

The Experience

The Real World Science Summer Teacher Seminar is an intense experience, proceeding as do most of the workshops described in this volume— a busy week of practicing activities, team building, and both on- and off-site activities. We have found that having a staff member experienced in science and STEM teaching has allowed us to make rigorous connections between history stories and WWII artifacts and national and local standards for science and STEM. In other words, it took our own use of an interdisciplinary team to create a valuable experience for interdisciplinary teachers.

Teachers begin by setting their goals, both individually and as a group. Every morning and afternoon session centers on a set of activities and pedagogical strategies, such as Driving Questions Boards and Question Formulation Technique. The teachers split their time between working in the museum's education classroom and its galleries. Teachers learn how to teach the science of buoyancy by learning about different types of landing craft, blood plasma, and penicillin while working next to an ambulance from WWII, and the science and technology behind the history of aviation while looking firsthand at different planes that flew during the war. The learning experiences are designed to challenge students to think about science topics in different ways, and the close interaction teachers gain with these macro-artifacts allows them to develop new pedagogical approaches to this information. Learning science with specific artifacts and stories from the past is as powerful as drawing social studies lessons from those things.

Time is dedicated to reflection and discussion at the end of every morning and afternoon session. Cohort members are asked how they will use the activities they have learned and how they plan to change their approaches based on what they gained, discussing how they can meet their own classroom requirements through new interdisciplinary approaches tied to the history of WWII. Teachers are excited by project-based learning, integrating literacy into their subject matter, and collaborating with colleagues teaching other subjects. They share strategies they can use with students and practice those strategies together during the sessions. Collaboratively building a mental model to carry into their science classrooms is enhanced through the exchange of ideas between their new-found colleagues.

Teacher workshops can be transformative for participants because they are taken outside normal experiences, introduced to new colleagues, and given resources that encourage them to rethink their practices. When a museum serves as the site of an immersive and engaging workshop, the potential for an educator's growth and transformation is all the greater. Many find that the model of best practices of science teaching in the workshop is more powerful than their previous experiences because it is connected to specific activities and stories. Seventy percent report they use more non-textbook sources of reading in class after the seminar. Participants unanimously report that the museum was a critical part of their learning experience, agreeing that if the seminar had been held in a hotel conference room or a convention center, it would not have been nearly as effective.

The Connections

We send our cohort home with new knowledge and skills, resources, and a set of colleagues to be part of their professional learning networks. Professional learning networks are key to teachers improving their practices. Connecting with other educators outside their own schools is crucial for teachers in our target audience, as they are often the only person teaching science at their grade level in their school. At least one-third of all our cohort members keep in regular communication with other members of their cohort, sharing ideas, resources, and professional development opportunities, and as friends. We also have social network accounts that we use to connect with them, so we can continue to support them after their time on-site concludes. We also connect cohort members across different years, introducing participating teachers to past members from their area and encouraging them to meet in person or virtually. Previous participants have served as important proxies for the museum's educational staff, representing the museum at events in regions across the country we cannot physically attend to share resources and offer support to other teachers within their communities. These professional networks are true of all teacher workshops at historical museums and sites. What in particular do we do to bolster their STEM connections?

1. Connect them with other institutions and individuals who can help them on this journey to successful interdisciplinary teaching. We provide them with many books published by the National Science Teaching Association. We give so many of these books as raffle prizes throughout the week that every teacher gets at least one (see a full list of titles at the end of this chapter).

2. Virtual visits from authors and experts on science pedagogy. These may vary from year to year, but usually include experts on the use of science notebooks, talk moves to encourage accountable talk, and structures for argumentative writing. Connecting them to these reliable sources of quality resources helps the teachers immediately, and places us as a source to whom they look for other valuable assets.

3. Investigate place-based learning, which is an idea allied to site-based learning. We model weaving the natural history and human history of a place together to enliven the teaching of important learning standards. On a visit to nearby City Park, we test the water quality of the lagoons, which are remnants of the city's wetland surroundings. City Park is also where one of Higgins Industries' first plants to build boats for WWII was located. We discuss the development of the region over geologic time and then the changes in recent human history. Traveling a little farther from the museum, we visit Lake Pontchartrain, where the Higgins boats were tested, and test the water quality there. We then talk about the locations of participants' schools and how they can use natural and historical sites near them to teach and learn. This has led to teachers in Washington visiting Hanford, where plutonium was generated for atomic weapons, and teachers in California visiting former airplane manufacturing plants with their students. It has led to teachers in Louisiana visiting farms where German prisoners of war worked during internment in WWII. This powerful teaching strategy cuts across disciplines, and our modeling of it makes us a trusted source for teachers.

Evaluation

For the first several years of the Real World Science Summer Teacher Seminar, we contracted an external evaluator to conduct an extensive evaluation. Everything from the quality of the curriculum and training to the accommodations and meals was evaluated using both surveys and interviews, with the evaluator on-site for the entire week. The evaluator regularly kept in touch with cohort members in the year following. When we found that 90 percent of the teachers were still using the curriculum and responding to surveys after a year, we changed our methods to keep in touch with them across the years. The teachers' thoughtful responses helped us improve every year, and those contacts and continued improvement kept them engaged with us.

We are now making a transition to running our own continuing evaluation of the program, using the tools left us by the evaluator, and focusing on areas we want to improve. Being able to share such strong data has helped us get support for the program and its expansion, internally within the institution and externally from our funding partner.

We are forming partnerships with institutions with aligned missions to conduct workshops with their on-site teacher programs. We worked with the National Flight Academy, a virtual reality learning program at the National Aviation Museum in Pensacola, Florida, to run shorter workshops there. Its location allowed us to use large artifacts to connect to STEM concepts as it does at our own site. There are missed opportunities to connect learning across disciplines—teaching history at STEM sites and teaching STEM at history sites. We are also working on finding ways to engage in virtual trainings, using videos of our galleries and artifacts to provide somewhat of the immersive experience of an on-site program.

Conclusion

We have successfully developed a program to support teachers in developing effective science teaching through the use of historical resources. By coming to our museum and learning how to use a curriculum tied to WWII, teachers become immersed in that history. The extensive engagement offered by the museum's workshops has improved the pedagogical practices of 150 teachers to date, and elevated the learning experiences of the many students they reach.

In our experience, teachers are enthusiastic about participating in interdisciplinary experiences, and funders are often interested in supporting them. The powerful connections across disciplines can be highly effective at improving learning experiences for both teachers and students. Interdisciplinary teaching can challenge the boundaries of learners' thinking and lead them into transformative experiences. There is a deep and compelling need to support teachers; museums and historical sites can help fill that need by offering teachers a place to learn new ways to engage with their students, as well as by sharing a museum's stories with new audiences. Museums of all specialties have much to offer to all teachers, no matter what they teach.

Contact Robert Wallace (rob.wallace@nationalww2museum.org) for copies of the evaluation reports of the Real World Science Summer Teacher Seminar.

REFERENCES

National Academies of Sciences, Engineering, and Medicine. *Science Teachers' Learning: Enhancing Opportunities, Creating Supportive Contexts.* Washington, DC: The National Academies Press, 2015. https://doi.org/10.17226/21836.

National Research Council. *A Framework for K–12 Science Education: Practices, Crosscutting Concepts, and Core Ideas.* Washington, DC: The National Academies Press, 2012 https://doi.org/10.17226/13165.

Real World Science curriculum: https://nationalww2museum.org/realworld science.

Books given to cohorts as reading resources with students:

Beaty, Andrea. 2013. *Rosie Revere, Engineer.* Illustrated edition. New York: Harry N. Abrams, 2013.

Bruchac, Joseph. *Code Talker: A Novel about the Navajo Marines of World War Two.* New York: Speak, an imprint of Penguin Random House, 2006.

Fries-Gaither, Jessica. *Exemplary Evidence: Scientists and Their Data.* Arlington, VA: National Science Teachers Association (NSTA) Press, 2019.

———. *Notable Notebooks: Scientists and Their Writings.* Arlington, VA: NSTA, Press, 2017.

Keeley, Page. *What Are They Thinking? Promoting Elementary Learning Through Formative Assessment.* Arlington, VA: NSTA Press, 2014.

Sheinkin, Steve. *Bomb: The Race to Build—and Steal—the World's Most Dangerous Weapon.* Illustrated edition. Bethel, OH: Flash Point, 2012.

Wheeler-Toppen, Jodi. *Once Upon a Life Science Book: 12 Interdisciplinary Activities to Create Confident Readers.* Arlington, VA: NSTA Press, 2010.

4.5

+

A Teacher's Perspective

Georgette Hackman

Georgette Hackman is a middle school teacher in Pennsylvania who shares here the connections that can be built through place-based professional development programs.

Professional development (PD) is a term that strikes either joy or fear in the hearts and minds of teachers. The reason for this is really quite simple. There are two types of PD: the kind that teachers are required to attend and the kind that is purely voluntary. School districts work hard to provide required PD that will help to achieve district goals and objectives, but that kind of PD doesn't always lead to profound change.

Place-based PD, on the other hand, has the power to both inspire and transform professional practice. I sought out my very first place-based PD opportunity ten years ago. It was a five-day summer teacher program that offered thirty teachers the opportunity to travel to George Washington's home to learn about his role in the founding of the US government. As an elementary school teacher, I didn't think I had the greatest odds of being chosen, but I decided to give it my best shot. I was selected to attend, and the rest, as they say, is history. The pre-conference readings were hard. The intimidation factor was huge. But that opportunity to stretch and grow captivated me and reminded me what I love most about teaching: learning!

The very best part was the people I met. Teaching can be lonely. We work in crowded schools, but most of our day is spent behind a closed door working with our students. In that first PD, I found my people. I discovered teachers who loved teaching, and was guided and encouraged

by education and museum professionals who made the commitment to
invest in educators.

In addition to the significant content that I learned that first week, I
was gifted with a new professional learning community. That connection
changed the trajectory of my career. Since that first, weeklong session, I
have traveled all over the country and even to foreign countries, each trip
funded or partially funded, to learn about a variety of topics in significant
historic spaces. Meeting teachers, scholars, and museum professionals
from around the country and the world is empowering. I learn new things
from each and every one. And more than anything, when I think that my
struggles are unique to me, I discover that we are all facing similar challenges. I discover that we are more alike than we are different. I discover
that, despite regional views and political beliefs, at the core, we are all
people who have committed our lives to teaching and learning. That common thread is transformational.

5

The Value of Evaluation

Christine Baron

Evaluation is easily the least exciting topic about which one can write. Encouraging institutions to engage in "robust" evaluations is one of the quickest ways to kill a good mood in just about any room. Trying to capture what teacher learning looks like at historic sites poses challenges that defy simple tools, such as Likert scale surveys (e.g., How engaging was your experience?) or market research, with which most museum professionals are familiar. In contrast, robust evaluation seeks to measure the shift in teachers' knowledge, attitudes, and perceptions following a site-based professional development experience. This book draws on and expands upon the findings of several quantitative and qualitative evaluation research projects undertaken at multiple historic sites from 2015 to 2019, including Thomas Jefferson's Monticello, George Washington's Mount Vernon, and Mystic Seaport Museum. This chapter looks at the complex circumstances in those projects that necessitated a nuanced approach to evaluation and discusses ways to develop future inquiries that build upon that research.

Challenges of Evaluating Teacher Learning at Historic Sites

Evaluating learning at historic sites offers a particular set of challenges because these sites are multisensory, interdisciplinary, and layered artifacts that present to the learner holistically. Within each of the three layers—the *textual, perceptual,* and *interpretive*—there are potential places to engage individuals in learning activities.[1] These layers hold true for recreational visitors as well as for teachers. Teachers, however, are a unique subset of adult visitors in that the purpose of their visit is to develop their own professional practice and to take their learning to an additional layer: the *external* layer. For teachers, that is the most important layer of the historic site: the external layer of the classroom, where they will apply what they have learned. Therefore, meaningful assessment and evaluation needs to focus on two key elements: the professional purpose of the teachers' visit and the ways in which they manage the transition of the information they gather on-site to their classrooms.

To understand what teachers take with them from the museum to their classrooms, let us begin consideration of teacher learning at the earliest point of contact for teachers coming on-site, be it in the parking lot, or at the front gate, or even on the website. Before any staff or interpretive text begins to mediate the experience, from the second visitors arrive, they begin to take in messages and assign meaning to what they see.[2]

Consider next what is generally experienced in a visit to a traditional house museum. The amount of information—cognitive, affective, and physical—encountered is overwhelming. Curated to a single moment in time are the artifacts of a (usually white) family of some note, typically with the accompanying wealth and social prominence that prompted concerned citizens to go about preserving the house. (Layered into these places now are the implicit and explicit values of those concerned citizens and their communities or organizations.) On display in the house are the signs and symbols of the family's social position, business interactions, and leisure activities (which belie the work of servants, enslaved or free, and the laborers, craftspeople, and others who made such lives possible). The grounds of such a house are similarly curated. Kitchen gardens sewn with heirloom seeds and farmland (minus the muck of livestock and large-scale labor) offer a meditation on the bucolic simplicity of days of yore (with nary a mention of contentious land deals between new settlers and indigenous populations, or the fate of other displaced peoples). While interpretive programming and media can offer nuanced and complex interpretations of the history of these spaces,[3] often, the degree to which one sees past a simple narrative of a benevolent, white, wealthy, upper-class family depends on one's position relative to that kind of family. This encapsulates the essential problem of evaluation of historic sites: if everyone begins their visit in a different relative position to a host of complex issues and ideas, how can the impact of interpretive programming be determined by the visit's end?

The complexity of this problem is amplified when the visit is part of a teacher professional development program. How does the programming offered help teachers shift their perspectives relative to that starting position *and help change classroom practice*? Does the exploration of these places reinforce existing dominant narratives, or does it help broaden or shift personal narratives, and if so, in what ways? And how can we compare that across multiple professional development programs held at multiple historic sites?

Much of our understanding of site-based teacher professional development (TPD) has been shaped by the lack of prior research on the effectiveness of museums in facilitating such programs. Unlike school systems, wherein large-scale, systemic, ongoing research projects are the norm, museums and historic sites largely operate as self-contained entities. The uniqueness and singularity of a historic place, which led to its preservation, is part of the barrier to identifying what is gained from interacting with it. The range of content, landscapes, structures, events, and collections varies so considerably that case studies and evaluations of single exhibits or programs are the research norm. As far back as 1995, as part of their attempt to develop a systematic research agenda for learning in museums, Falk and Dierking identified the focus of previous research on "short-term studies assessing the in-museum behavior or exit knowledge of visitors"[4] as both evidence of and an inhibiting factor in defining generalizable information about the kind of learning that museums facilitate.

In our work assessing what teachers gained from historic site-based professional development (HSBPD) programs, we employed Q-Methodology, a research method designed to register subtle subjective shifts in individual perceptions on a range of issues. The items we developed for teachers' responses, referred to as the concourse,[5] related to the professional lives and work of teachers. By focusing on teachers' professional needs rather than their visitor experiences, we were able to move beyond the singularity of a specific historic site to allow for findings that would hold across other similar sites and teacher education programs. This series of studies was intended to provide a *broad foundation* from which to build further evaluations / research at historic sites in order to develop a deeper understanding of what teachers learn from them. To move forward from this work, it is not necessary to continue to use Q-Methodology or other broad-based evaluative tools. Rather, it is essential to engage in more targeted inquiries grounded in questions of learning related to teachers' professional lives.

Layers of Historic Sites

To engage in these more targeted investigations, it is necessary to consider to what layer of a historic site teachers are responding and how they are making meaning of it. Each layer of a historic site poses different pedagogical questions and opportunities. Situating evaluation within the proper layer ensures that the right questions are being asked and that those questions will generate meaningful answers.

Textual Layer

Using a very broad definition of text as "representations that people generate or use to make meaning either for themselves or others,"[6] the *textual layer* of the site includes the peculiar configuration of the natural and built environment—the "what" of the place—that defines the site. In most historic places, there is a visual tangle of old and new, restored, replaced, and missing that provides an anthology of historical and contemporary texts the visitor encounters. Here, the primary pedagogical questions concern text assessment, identification, classification, and enumeration. For example, in archeology-oriented programs, questions might include, *What is this?* and *Where did it come from?* While it might constitute the first element of an investigation, in the context of a historic site, rarely would text assessment be the sole focus of public or educational programing, as questions of identification and classification will lead to interpretive questions about the nature, function, and validity of such schemes. The urge to move toward meaning-making, to understand *why* humans created this text in this way, speaks to the constraints of the textual layer but also to an essential distinction necessary when we speak of *history*: there is a difference between the past (the evidence that remains) and our interpretation of it (the products of investigation of the evidence).[7] Thus, the textual layer functions as the available evidence for investigation, without interpretation or interaction.

While it is essential to understand what constitutes a historic place, as that delineates and provides context for future study, it is not enough to know the inert text of it, which is why we need to understand how we, as humans, make meaning of it: the perceptual and interpretive layers.

Perceptual Layer

The *perceptual layer* is how we make sense of the place through our sensory experiences. Questions of learning posed within this layer center on learning at historic sites, in response to and in concert with the place and its components. The complex interplay of cognitive engagement, affective experiences, and physical sensations and experiences plays a considerable role in perceptions of the site.[8]

Questions of learning in the perceptual layer center on the myriad ways individuals think, feel, or experience the information gathered during their interaction with a place. What do they now understand from being in that place that they did not before? How does seeing the sweep of the land explain why certain battlefield positions would be advantageous? How does seeing the interplay of space, light, sound, smell, and so on, shape conceptions of historical agents' lives, and of their humanity? What navigational or sensory challenges affect how people interact with the site? Many of the ideas about disciplinary learning in history that draw upon cognitive and affective theories (e.g., historical thinking, historical empathy) and dominate K–12 teaching and learning are situated questions in this layer of the historic site, offering immediate bridges between the historic site and those formal education spaces.

Interpretive Layer

Finally, the *interpretive layer* of historic sites, in which we ascribe meaning to the place, offers two complicating problems for learning at historic sites: the subjectivities of visitors and the ill-structured problem space of the historic site.

Independent of interpretive media or programs provided by the site, individuals visiting historic places use their prior knowledge about the site and its persons, events, and history, along with personal experiences, identities, histories, and innumerable other issues, to seek from and assign meaning to these complex spaces. In this way, every historic site requires of its visitors a consideration of their own multiple identities relative to the history they encounter. What visitors learn from the experience, in large measure, depends on their willingness or ability to consider lives different from their own. They may be guided through the space by site staff, whose own subjectivities and preferred interpretations of its history play a significant role in how visitors interpret the site.[9]

The Ill-Structured Problem Space

Individuals then encounter the historic site itself. Ill-structured problems have multiple possible answers, no definitive path to a solution, and unknown elements, such as missing or unavailable evidence,[10] which differentiates historic sites and their directed learning activities from other informal learning spaces. Consider two typical activities offered in different informal spaces: working at the water tables found at a science center and writing with a quill pen at a historic place. While both activities offer visitors enjoyable hands-on activity, they are not of the same kind. Working at the water table demonstrates a transferable principle—buoyancy—necessary for exploring larger scientific questions; writing with the quill pen offers an opportunity to use the technology of an earlier age, with little applicability beyond that.

What if one adjusts these activities to be parallel, posing a "scientific question" versus a "historical question"? For example, "Will it sink or float? (What is buoyancy?)," or "Was the battle of Lexington and Concord really a battle?"[11] Whatever the visitor's age, background, ethnicity, or prior experiences, the water table is universal: no matter who uses it, the item will either sink or float, with predictable results, demonstrating the principles of buoyancy.

Conversely, if one surveys the site at Lexington Green or wanders along Battle Road at Minuteman National Historic Site in Concord, Massachusetts, it is first necessary to situate the place historiographically, disregarding the modern intrusions—roadways, parking lots, rest areas—that provide visitor comfort but change the historical landscape. The question of whether Lexington and Concord was really a battle offers an opportunity to consider a range of questions that might include: Whose account of the events do you have? Whose are missing? Which account might be more compelling or accurate? Why might you believe one source over another's account of the event? These and many other questions can be raised, but the available documentary and physical evidence offers no definitive conclusion.

Beyond the historical sources and the site itself, the individuals who engage with them will bring their own lenses to the interpretation. Military, civilian, and pacifist perspectives will differ sharply. British and American visitors might feel compelled to support the positions of those who fought on "their" side. Young children might notice how the firefight took place very close to nearby homes, identifying with how scary the events must have been for the children who lived there. No matter how the event is presented, the complexities of individual visitors' multiple identities must be addressed within questions of learning at historic sites. Further, one must wrestle with historical questions that are interpreted and reinterpreted as new evidence emerges and are rarely, if ever, definitively settled. Thus, in addition to the changing response to historical questions posed by the evidence, the perspective from which individuals interpret the questions changes the outcome.

Thus, questions of learning, in addition to considering perceptual experiences, require an acknowledgment of the factors that influence the ways in which individuals resolve these historical questions, in mediated and unmediated ways. For example, evaluating teacher learning in this layer can focus on what specific content was taken from an exhibit or tour. Rather than looking for discrete facts (e.g., details of the Lewis and Clark Expedition), it would be more beneficial to ask about the evolution of the visitor's thinking related to particular concepts over the course of their experience with the exhibit. Gathering data on and tying outcomes to a range of demographic information—grade level, type of school, years of teachers' experience and education, and so on—that was used in our analysis of the sites, is necessary to fully understand the perspective from which teachers are viewing the exhibit.

The External Layer of Historic Sites: Teachers' Classrooms

Unlike most other visitors, the purpose of teachers' work in HSBPD is to improve their professional practice. Doing so in an HSBPD program means doing so alongside and in conversation with peer professionals. These peer professionals all bring the previously indicated subjectivities and experiences with them, as well as another critically important perspective: they view the historic place in pedagogical terms and with the needs of their particular students in mind.[12] Peer teachers provide another layer of teacher learning in HSBPD, and interaction with them is often a considerable part of participating teachers' rationale for attending.[13]

As the larger purpose of their visit is to deepen their professional practice in their own classrooms as individual teachers, this shifts the question of learning toward how individuals transfer knowledge.[14] Therefore, questions of teacher learning at historic sites should look at how they intend to use the materials and information gleaned from their experiences at the site in order to position research and evaluation from an individual, cognitive perspective.

The goal in many HSBPD programs is to generate lessons for teachers to use in their classrooms, based on deeper understandings about the site. This professional development model assumes that teachers approach HSBPD as a means to solve a problem, namely the teacher's self-identified need to improve their knowledge and skills related to a particular historical era/person/event. Looking at how a teacher develops a resource for students shows how they manage the transition of the information they gather on-site back to their classrooms,[15] and offers the most direct look at what content, materials, and practices gained on-site actually change classroom practice. This means that to understand what teachers are taking from the site, it is necessary to look at the *process*, rather than the *products*, of lesson development as a mental effort that is unlikely to be repeated in the same way with subsequent lessons, historical content, or conundrums. Here again, understanding how teachers construct lessons in aggregate, rather than the individual content contained in a single lesson or set of lessons, brings insights into the support that teachers need to translate the materials found on-site into meaningful classroom curriculum.

Conclusion

Evaluating teachers' work in HSBPD is essential for understanding what teachers learn on-site and bring back to their classrooms. To engage in meaningful evaluation, it is necessary to understand and work within challenges posed by the complex layers of historic sites. Above all, it is critical to remember that the most important layer of the historic site for teachers is the external layer of their classroom. It is there that the work of professional development ultimately succeeds or fails.

NOTES

1. For more detail on these "layers," see Genevieve Bell and Paul Dourish, "Getting Out of the City: Meaning and Structure in Everyday Encounters with Space," Workshop on Ubiquitous Computing on the Urban Frontier at Ubicomp, Nottingham, UK, September 2004; M. A. Callanan, "Conducting Cognitive Developmental Research in Museums: Theoretical Issues and Practical Considerations," *Journal of Cognition and Development* 13 (2012): 137–51; M. Carmona, S. Tiesdell, T. Heath, and T. Oc, *Public Places — Urban Spaces: The Dimensions of Urban Design*, second edition (Oxford: Architectural Press, 2010); O. J. Dwyer and D. H. Alderman, "Memorial Landscapes: Analytic Questions and Metaphors," *GeoJournal* 73 (2008): 165–78; D. Drozdzewski, S. De Nardi, and E. Waterton, "Geographies of Memory, Place and Identity: Intersections in Remembering War and Conflict," *Geography Compass* 10 (2016): 447–56.

2. Z. D. Doering and A. J. Pekarik, "Questioning the Entrance Narrative," *Journal of Museum Education* 21, no. 3 (1996): 20–25.

3. R. Handler and E. Gable, *The New History in an Old Museum: Creating the Past at Colonial Williamsburg* (Durham: Duke University Press, 1997); C. Lewis, *The Changing Face of Public History: The Chicago Historical Society and the Transformation of an American Museum* (DeKalb: Northern Illinois University Press, 2005); J. K. Tchen, "Creating a Dialogic Museum: The Chinatown History Museum Experiment," in *Museums and Communities: The Politics of Public Culture*, eds. I. Karp, C. M. Kreamer, and S. D. Lavine, 285–326 (Washington, DC: Smithsonian Institution Press, 1992).

4. J. H. Falk and L. D. Dierking (eds.), *Public Institutions for Personal Learning: Establishing a Research Agenda* (Washington, DC: American Association of Museums, 1995), 9.

5. The full concourse from the 2017 study can be found at teacherinsites.org.

6. Suzanne E. Wade and Elizabeth Birr Moje, "The Role of Text in Classroom Learning," *Handbook of Reading Research* 3 (2000): 609–27.

7. Bruce A. VanSledright, "What Does It Mean to Think Historically . . . and How Do You Teach It?," *Social Studies Today: Research and Practice* 68, no. 3 (2010): 112–20.

8. Lisa Zachrich, Allison Weller, Christine Baron, and Christiane Bertram, "Historical Experiences: A Framework for Encountering Complex Historical Sources," *History Education Research Journal* 17, no. 2 (2020): 243–75.

9. Derek Alderman and Rachel M. Campbell, "Symbolic Excavation and the Artifact Politics of Remembering Slavery in the American South: Observations from Walterboro, South Carolina," *Southeastern Geographer* 48, no. 3 (2008): 338–55; E. Arnold Modlin, Derek H. Alderman, and Glenn W. Gentry, "Tour Guides as

Creators of Empathy: The Role of Affective Inequality in Marginalizing the Enslaved at Plantation House Museum." *Tourist Studies* 11, no. 1 (2011): 3–19.

10. Jean E. Pretz,, Adam J. Naples, and Robert J. Sternberg, "Recognizing, Defining, and Representing Problems," in *The Psychology of Problem Solving*, eds. J. E. Davidson and R. J. Sternberg, 3–30 (Cambridge: Cambridge University Press, 1999); Min Kyu Kim, "Theoretically Grounded Guidelines for Assessing Learning Progress: Cognitive Changes in Ill-Structured Complex Problem Solving Contexts," *Educational Technology Research and Development* 60, no. 4 (2012): 601–22; James F. Voss, S. Tyler, and L. Yengo, "Individual Differences in the Solving of Social Science Problems," in *Individual Differences in Cognition*, eds. R. Dillon and R. Schmeck, 205–32 (Cambridge, MA: Academic Press, 1983).

11. Sam Wineburg, Daisy Martin, and Chauncey Monte-Sano, *Reading Like a Historian: Teaching Literacy in Middle and High School History Classrooms* (New York: Teachers College Press, 2011).

12. Christine Baron, "Understanding Historical Thinking at Historic Sites," *Journal of Educational Psychology* 104, no. 3 (2012): 833–47, doi:10.1037/ a0027476.

13. Christine Baron, Sherri Sklarwitz, Hyeyoung Bang, and Hanadi Shatara, "Understanding what Teachers Gain from Professional Development at Historic Sites," *Theory & Research in Social Education* 47, no. 1 (2019): 76–107.

14. Christine Baron, "Structuring Historic Site-Based History Laboratories for Teacher Education," *Journal of Museum Education* 39 (2014): 10–19; S. M. Barnett and S. J. Ceci, "When and Where Do We Apply What We Learn?: A Taxonomy for Far Transfer," *Psychological Bulletin* 128 (2002): 612–37, doi:10.1037//0033 -2909.128.4.612; J. G. Greeno and Y. Engstrom, "Learning in Activity," in *The Cambridge Handbook of the Learning Sciences*, eds. by R. K. Sawyer, 128–50 (Cambridge: Cambridge University Press, 2014).

15. Pretz, Naples, and Sternberg, "Recognizing, Defining, and Representing Problems."

REFERENCES

Alderman, Derek, and Rachel M. Campbell. "Symbolic Excavation and the Artifact Politics of Remembering Slavery in the American South: Observations from Walterboro, South Carolina." *Southeastern Geographer* 48, no. 3 (2008): 338–55.

Barnett, S. M., and S. J. Ceci. "When and Where Do We Apply What We Learn?: A Taxonomy for Far Transfer." *Psychological Bulletin* 128 (2002): 612–37. doi:10.1037//0033-2909.128.4.612.

Baron, Christine. "Structuring Historic Site-Based History Laboratories for Teacher Education." *Journal of Museum Education* 39 (2014): 10–19.

———. "Understanding Historical Thinking at Historic Sites." *Journal of Educational Psychology* 104, no. 3 (2012): 833–47. doi:10.1037/ a0027476.

Baron, Christine, Sherri Sklarwitz, Hyeyoung Bang, and Hanadi Shatara. "Understanding What Teachers Gain from Professional Development at Historic Sites." *Theory & Research in Social Education* 47, no. 1 (2019): 76–107.

Bell, G., and P. Dourish. "Getting Out of the City: Meaning and Structure in Everyday Encounters with Space." Workshop on Ubiquitous Computing on the Urban Frontier at Ubicomp, Nottingham, UK, September 2004.

Bitgood, S. "What Do We Know about School Field Trips?" In *What Research Says about Learning in Science Museums*, volume 2, edited by R. J. Hannapel, 12–16. Washington, DC: Association of Science-Technology Centers, 1994.

Callanan, M. A. "Conducting Cognitive Developmental Research in Museums: Theoretical Issues and Practical Considerations." *Journal of Cognition and Development* 13 (2012): 137–51. doi:10.1080/15248372.2012.666730.

Carmona, M., S. Tiesdell, T. Heath, and T. Oc. *Public Places—Urban Spaces: The Dimensions of Urban Design*. Second edition. Oxford: Architectural Press, 2010.

Doering, Z. D., and A. J. Pekarik. "Questioning the Entrance Narrative." *Journal of Museum Education* 21, no. 3 (1996): 20–25.

Drozdzewski, D., S. De Nardi, and E. Waterton. "Geographies of Memory, Place and Identity: Intersections in Remembering War and Conflict," *Geography Compass* 10 (2016): 447–56.

Dudzinska-Przesmitzki, D., and R. S. Grenier. "Nonformal and Informal Adult Learning in Museums: A Literature Review." *The Journal of Museum Education* 33 (2008): 9–22.

Dwyer, O. J., and D. H. Alderman. "Memorial Landscapes: Analytic Questions and Metaphors." *GeoJournal* 73 (2008): 165–78.

Falk, J. H., and L. D. Dierking, eds. *Public Institutions for Personal Learning: Establishing a Research Agenda*. Washington, DC: American Association of Museums, 1995.

Greeno, J. G., and Y. Engstrom. "Learning in Activity," In *The Cambridge Handbook of the Learning Sciences*, edited by R. K. Sawyer, 128–50. Cambridge: Cambridge University Press, 2014.

Handler, R., and E. Gable. *The New History in an Old Museum: Creating the Past at Colonial Williamsburg*. Durham: Duke University Press, 1997.

Lewis, C. *The Changing Face of Public History: The Chicago Historical Society and the Transformation of an American Museum*. DeKalb: Northern Illinois University Press, 2005.

Min Kyu Kim, "Theoretically Grounded Guidelines for Assessing Learning Progress: Cognitive Changes in Ill-Structured Complex ProblemSolving Contexts." *Educational Technology Research and Development* 60, no. 4 (2012): 601–22.

Modlin, E. Arnold, Derek H. Alderman, and Glenn W. Gentry. "Tour Guides as Creators of Empathy: The Role of Affective Inequality in Marginalizing the Enslaved at Plantation House Museums." *Tourist Studies* 11, no. 1 (April 2011): 3–19.

Pretz, Jean E., Adam J. Naples, and Robert J. Sternberg. "Recognizing, Defining, and Representing Problems." In *The Psychology of Problem Solving*, edited by J. E. Davidson and R. J. Sternberg, 3–30. Cambridge: Cambridge University Press, 1999.

Tchen, J. K. "Creating a Dialogic Museum: The Chinatown History Museum Experiment." In *Museums and Communities: The Politics of Public Culture*, edited by I. Karp, C. M. Kreamer, and S. D. Lavine, 285–326. Washington, DC: Smithsonian Institution Press, 1992.

VanSledright, Bruce A. "What Does It Mean to Think Historically . . . and How Do You Teach It?." *Social Studies Today: Research and Practice* 68, no. 3 (2010): 112–20.

Voss, James F., S. Tyler, and L. Yengo. "Individual Differences in the Solving of Social Science Problems." In *Individual Differences in Cognition*, edited by R. Dillon and R. Schmeck, 205–32. Cambridge, MA: Academic Press, 1983.

Wade, Suzanne E., and Elizabeth Birr Moje. "The Role of Text in Classroom Learning." *Handbook of Reading Research* 3 (2000): 609–27.

Wineburg, Sam, Daisy Martin, and Chauncey Monte-Sano. *Reading Like a Historian: Teaching Literacy in Middle and High School History Classrooms.* New York: Teachers College Press, 2011.

Zachrich, Lisa, Allison Weller, Christine Baron, and Christiane Bertram. "Historical Experiences: A Framework for Encountering Complex Historical Sources." *History Education Research Journal* 17, no. 2 (2020): 243–75.

II

+

PRACTICE

6

Setting Goals

The Crucial First Step in Creating Your Museum's Teacher Professional Development Program

Mike Adams

Over the past few years, I have created, consulted on, facilitated, and evaluated more than 120 teacher professional development (TPD) programs in a wide range of formats, in-person and online, at museums, schools, and other educational settings, reaching thousands of teachers around the country. The planning process for every single program started the same way: with a reflective exercise exploring institutional goals and resources. Everything else is built on that foundation.

Positioned in this book at the transition from the conceptual frameworks for effective TPD to actually building a program, this chapter focuses on two fundamental considerations at the outset of planning TPD:

1. The museum's specific goals for TPD (Why are *we* creating TPD?)
2. The museum's inventory of TPD-specific resources (Do we have the things we need to do this right?)

Much of what makes effective museum TPD stems from the institution-specific responses to these considerations. They define the museum's identity as a TPD provider. They communicate the purpose of TPD to internal and external stakeholders. And they inform choices about program format, teacher cohorts, and the rest of the decision-making outlined in this handbook. In short, they are the core of the goal-setting process. Given the considerable financial, staffing, and other commitments TPD requires, it is worth taking the time to set clear goals at the beginning of the process.

This chapter offers two sets of reflective questions. The first set addresses goal-setting: Why are *we* creating TPD? Having made it this far, you know why museums, in general, should offer TPD. At this stage, however, it is imperative to be able to articulate why *your* museum, specifically, is engaging in this important work. The second set of questions addresses what the museum is positioned to offer: Do we have the things we need to do this right? In other words: What is available to you, and what do you need to secure in order to build an effective program?

There are no categorically "right" answers. But by addressing these questions now, you will build a solid foundation and clear sense of direction for future decision-making. You should be able to confidently answer them before committing to any specific elements of your program. For each question, I provide suggestions for the types of things to consider.

I strongly recommend writing down your responses. It makes for better reflective practice before, during, and after you build (and run) the program. And I promise that, at some point, someone in your organization, probably someone financially minded, will ask, "Why are we doing this, again?" Better to have the answers at your fingertips.

Let's get started.

Why Are We Creating TPD?

1. What is your museum's mission? This seems a bit cliché, but it's important. Start by thinking about your mission, and how you can be on track for building TPD that benefits your museum.
2. What is your museum's education framework? TPD should reflect your museum's interpretive methodologies. How do you teach, and why do you teach that way? Are there "pillars," key components, or core elements of your museum's educational approach? If your museum had an "education mission statement," what would it be? Articulating this framework is essential for creating TPD that works for your museum. It also empowers you to communicate your identity as a TPD provider to teachers, guest scholars, partner organizations, and other stakeholders.
3. What are the education-specific priorities of your museum? Beyond the obvious goal of teaching the content your museum interprets, are there initiatives with which TPD might be aligned? Are there measurable impacts the TPD might have, for example, 25 percent increase in bookings for a field trip program, 100 percent increase in lesson plan downloads, recruiting ten teachers for your advisory board, and so on?
4. What site-specific content do you want to teach that you are not currently teaching in another program? What sets TPD apart from

programs teachers could already attend, such as your lecture series or a group tour?

5. What transferable skills might teachers gain from your TPD programs? Is there a research, interpretive, or teaching strategy your museum uses to great effect that might translate into meaningful classroom instruction?

6. Who are the teachers you want to engage? How many teachers? How many students do you hope to indirectly serve? Is there a region you want to have represented? If you say "local" or "regional," define that term. What grade levels of educators would benefit most? HINT: The answer is not "K–12." How are applicable education standards aligned with the content and skills you teach? Demographics: lengths of teaching tenures; race and ethnicity; gender identity; types of schools represented; Title 1 status; on-level, accelerated, or AP teachers; etc.? Psychographics: preexisting knowledge, professional goals, learning preferences, etc.?

7. Do you need to use existing, or generate new, revenue? Do you need to consider both earned and contributed revenue? If funding is "in-hand," what conditions need to be satisfied? If you are seeking funding, what are the expectations of the potential revenue source? Does the TPD need to be sustainable beyond the initial program or funding cycle?

8. What kinds of relationships do you want to build? At its core, TPD is about relationship-building. Are you building relationships with individual teachers, schools, districts, other education agencies, or some combination of these? What might those relationships look like?

Go back and read your responses. Look for connections, themes, and trends. From these, draft goals or objectives using any format that works for you. Write them down. Make sure everyone involved with the TPD understands the goals. Think of these as mini elevator pitches for TPD. Here are three examples:

- "Highlighting the museum's new, in-exhibit, digital interactives and using our approach to teaching student voice through primary source analysis, the TPD will create new relationships with thirty middle school social studies teachers from a fifty-mile radius. There will be a 50 percent increase in bookings for our grant-funded field trip next school year."
- "We are doing TPD to use the balance of a grant received to reinterpret our orientation gallery. The TPD will engage twenty experienced high school social studies teachers from schools with predominantly

black student populations throughout the country who will create new, online resources for the museum."

- "The TPD will engage twenty-five teachers in grades 5 through 12, representing approximately 1,800 students from the St. Olaf School District. This introduces new audiences to our content while providing feedback from the local teaching community to support development of future educational initiatives."

If this step is difficult, revisit your answers. Again, there are no "right" answers. But your responses should feel like part of a coherent whole. You should be able to confidently respond to the question, "Why should *we* do this?" Once you can articulate why *your* museum is creating TPD, take stock of what your museum can commit to this important work.

Do We Have the Things We Need to Do This Right?

The previous section addressed the "why" part of the reflective exercise. This section addresses the "how, what, where, and when." The answers to these questions create your TPD inventory. This is your way of being able to communicate to internal and external stakeholders what your museum is positioned to offer and what it still needs. If this feels like a lot, it is. Creating TPD that is fun, interesting, and engaging is a sprint. Creating TPD that is all of those things *and* effective is a marathon. These are certainly not all the things you will need to consider, but they are some of the most important. To get the "right" answers for *your* museum, your responses to *each* of the following questions should include *who* will do the work, how much *time* can be dedicated to this aspect of TPD, and what *resources* can be allocated (consider direct and indirect costs).

1. Who will be in charge of the TPD? Your project lead needs to be someone with highly developed executive function. This person should be a "big picture" thinker who understands organizational needs and possesses a strong working knowledge of classroom education. It helps immeasurably if the project lead can also develop and deliver tours, workshops, and other program components. Choose carefully.
2. Who makes up the rest of the TPD team? Note that some of these roles can be filled by the same person/people, for example, your project lead might also be your andragogy and evaluation expert.
   a. Who are your content experts? What roles will they play in identifying, approving, and delivering content? If you bring in outside experts, how might that affect the project timeline, budget, etc.?

b. Who are your andragogy experts? Who makes sure you use best practices in working with adult learners?

c. Who are your pedagogy experts? Teachers need to be able to apply what they learn from your TPD in their own practice. You and they need someone who speaks their "language."

d. Who is your evaluation expert? If this person is not in-house, where can you find someone?

e. Who else (inside the organization) might play a role in the TPD? Consider all potential contributors outside the education department: marketing, development, facilities, security, etc. When should they be brought into the conversation?

f. Who else (outside the organization) might play a role in the TPD? Are there partner organizations or individuals who might enhance the program?

3. How will teachers find out about your program?

a. What is the status of your current network of educators? Do you have a database of educators who might be interested?

b. What ways can you recruit teachers? What marketing tools do you have? Think about all contact points—online, in person, mail, etc.

c. Who might help if you need recruitment support? Think about district-level administrators, local or state education agencies, professional education organizations, and internal contributors like the group sales team, admissions staff, board members, etc.

4. What can your museum provide? This section emphasizes your institution's "museumness." When creating effective TPD, as with any educational experience, your museum's exhibits, programs, and resources are best thought of as tools—means to achieve educational ends—hence the placement of these questions so late in the process.

a. What programs, exhibits, and on-site activities will you include? What specific content will you teach? What will the teachers actually see and do? Experiences that feel special make for impactful TPDs. Can you offer behind-the-scenes experiences? Can you get an A-list speaker? What resources in your geographic area could enhance the TPD?

b. What other educational resources do you have? What are the takeaways? Think of print materials—lesson plans, posters, etc.—as well as online resources. Also consider things that aren't teacher-specific. Can you offer a one-year membership to the museum or provide premier access to other programs throughout the year?

c. Can you provide official, reportable professional development credit? Do you need to?[1]

     d. What time of year can you offer TPD? During the school year? Weekends? Summer? Does this work for the teachers you hope to engage?[2]

     e. What times of day can you offer TPD? Can the program run before/after the museum opens to the public? Are there experiences that need to happen while the museum is open? Do these times work for teachers?

     f. What direct costs can you cover for teachers? Lower costs equal greater interest and more equitable access. For an afterschool TPD, you need to provide dinner. For a residential summer TPD, airfare and hotel stays are logical costs to cover; but what about airport parking and transfers, baggage fees, etc.? Does lunch need to be brought in or can teachers go out? What about breakfast? How do you keep coffee cups full? These costs add up fast. Do you have organizational policies that restrict reimbursements/payment for nonemployees?

     g. What nonexhibit spaces can you use for TPD? Do you have classroom space? How might the space's characteristics affect program capacity, the types of activities you can do, etc.? Are there opportunity costs involved in using this room for TPD?

     h. How will teachers get to you? If the TPD is a residential program, where will the teachers stay? Regardless of program format, if teachers drive, where will they park, and who pays for it?

You probably noticed the questions above became increasingly detail-oriented. In fact, looking at these questions in reverse, you may notice an order reminiscent of Maslow's (controversial but well-known and popularly acknowledged) hierarchy of needs. This is intentional. When building a program, it is important to think holistically about what your museum is positioned to offer. Asking, "Where will teachers park their cars?" is an important part of this process. But if your goal is to create effective TPD, that question is not the best place to start.

Turning Goals into Decisions

When I sat down to write this, I was torn between two cliché analogies with which I wanted to open the chapter. The first involved the line from preflight safety announcements about securing your own mask before assisting others. The other had to do with embarking on a journey and needing to know where you are before you can know where you're going. Both felt particularly clumsy and overused. But both are appropriate for thinking about goal-setting for TPD. The museum needs to have an institutional goal that TPD will be effective for all its stakeholders, especially the museum itself. And it needs to know what it has and what it needs to consider before taking the next steps of "Building a Program."

As you will find in the following chapters, there are many more considerations than those outlined here. But now you have a solid foundation: your museum's TPD-provider identity, a vision for what you want to accomplish, and an inventory of the resources available to ensure success. You are ready to move forward. Get building.

NOTES

1. In my professional experience, this need is overstated in the museum field. Teachers participate in TPD for myriad reasons, especially TPD from external providers like museums. If you can provide reportable hours, or partner with an accredited provider, without committing much time or energy, great. If not, it will not be a deal-breaker for the majority of teachers. Java Robinson, "Why Professional Development Matters," National Education Agency, February 11, 2019, https://www.nea.org/professional-excellence/student-engagement/tools -tips/why-professional-development-matters; *Teachers Know Best: Teachers' Views on Professional Development*, study by the Bill & Melinda Gates Foundation, January–March 2014, https://s3.amazonaws.com/edtech-production/reports /Gates-PDMarketResearch-Dec5.pdf; American Institutes for Research: District and School Improvement Center, *Guide to Working with External Partners*, fourth edition, April 2019, https://www.air.org/sites/default/files/downloads/report /Guide-to-Working-with-External-Providers-4th-DSI-April-2019.pdf.

2. Consider, for instance, the start and end dates of the school year. An early August summer institute might be fine for teachers from New England and the Mid-Atlantic. But you'll exclude teachers from the Southeast and west of the Mississippi. Drew Desilver, "'Back to School' Means Anytime from Late July to after Labor Day, Depending on Where in the US You Live," Pew Research Center, August 14, 2019, https://www.pewresearch.org/fact-tank/2019/08/14/back-to -school-dates-u-s/.

7

✛

Effective Teacher Professional Development Program Design

Allison Wickens

The variety of teacher programs being offered by history museums and historic sites is immense, and the formats range from thirty-minute digital confidence builders to immersive multiday residential experiences. They cover historical content from across the centuries and around the world. This chapter outlines two salient formats to explore and four key elements in program design. Addressing each element will ensure that your program, no matter the format, provides a strong connection to your site's mission and gives the participants the bandwidth, tools, and incentive to apply what they learn to their classrooms. Bolstered by the guiding strategies in other chapters of this book, these program components are intended to inspire and align with all the work your institution does for and with schools.

Selecting a format for your program can be a creative opportunity. Instead of thinking of program formats as limiting constraints, imposed-upon mandates, or intimidating barriers, lean into the strengths and opportunities each type of program offers. Formats, including online, afterschool, multiday, semester-long series, and printed resources, must balance institutional assets and mandates, audience needs, and resources. Whether reinvigorating a long-time program that has shifted into neutral or starting from zero with a newly funded program, being intentional about your format allows you to honor the fluidity between your institution and the teachers you serve. Whatever your format, a great match exists if you design with intent.

To start, this chapter highlights two program types that provide opportunities for the reach and impact of your work for schools to go beyond your walls. Digital programs (live or asynchronous) and sustained programs (multiday or series) present outreach and relationship-building strategies that may inspire investment in these approaches. Even if your program format is different from these two examples, think about how digital or sustained engagements can improve upon your chosen format. The second half of this chapter will provide a practical checklist for key elements to include that will strengthen every professional development (PD) program you create, regardless of its format. "Site Experience" ensures the uniqueness of your PD project; "Historical Focus" establishes your institution's expertise; "Classroom Applicability" scaffolds effective transference to the formal learning world outside your PD; and "Reflection" builds continuity and trust among your institution, your training experiences, and the audiences you serve.

Digital Programs

Whether you have a program that has been adapted to be delivered online or was digitally born, you have a slate of different tools to use to support teachers. Understanding the strengths of your digital format will help you sustain impact while reaching audiences in new ways. At George Washington's Mount Vernon, we designed our Slavery in George Washington's World Digital Symposium (fall 2020) based on the successes and challenges of our summer 2020 digitally adapted program. The program, scheduled across a weekend, had twenty speakers over three days. Each evening session served as a culminating keynote to the themed sessions presented during the day. Sessions alternated among speakers who could provide deep historical content, transferrable classroom application, and virtual tours of key locations at Mount Vernon that helped to tell the story of enslavement. A dedicated interactive website allowed the hundreds of participants to share their reflections and comments with others in real time, and to access past recordings in order to participate in some elements asynchronously.

Keep Your Site at the Center

Site-based experiences are incredibly important to bring to an online PD session. If you cannot host directly from your historic spaces or signature exhibitions, then you should actively integrate into the program images, videos, and other digital assets created at your site or that highlight your collection. Use language that immerses online participants in your space and connects them emotionally to the experience on-site. They should feel like they know your site and what makes it a special resource for them, even after a digital encounter. At Mount Vernon, we record video tours of the grounds or use our virtual tour to showcase specific locations so that even as we deliver the program from an office cubical, the participants hear and see our authentic experiences in the historic spaces we interpret. Phrases like "walk in footsteps" or "hearing the birds around us" simulate the sensory experiences of being on-site.

Don't Fear the Silence Online

While leading online sessions, the biggest barrier to reflective activities is often a compelling need to fill silence, but the space given, after a reflective prompt, should honor the gravity intended by the question you asked. Coach your scholars and content experts in this practice as well. Learning online can feel relentless if presenters are rushing. This can be challenging since many presenters traditionally rely on feedback from a live audience to guide their pacing and pauses. You may not see chatting or questions at the rate you do in person, but you should trust that learning is still happening though responses are subdued.

Construct Asynchronous Avenues for Reflection and Contribution

Program content online can sometimes march forward, and without the ability to "rewind," opportunities to reflect quickly come and go. Participants don't exist in a shared physical space and are often pulled in multiple directions when they tune in. A dedicated webpage or shared drive where participants can always go to access and contribute to past content can help them internalize the information. Reflection should happen at the time that is most conducive to the participant, not the time most convenient for you. For greatest effectiveness, record your sessions and, if permissions are secured, share these recordings with future trainings too.

Aggregate Comments and Questions

Support group reflection and invite shared debriefing by taking the time to analyze and share a high-level view of the questions and discussions that are happening during an online session. When in person, this process is largely audible to all involved, but it takes more intention by the program planner in the digital world. As the program facilitator, you may have the best view of all the input coming in through multiple digital channels.

Right-Size Your Sessions and Programs

Build your content sessions with an eye for shorter bursts of varied content interwoven with different media sources. Attendees of digital professional development have the freedom to explore the ideas presented during your program by simultaneously browsing related content on the internet. They may also be cooking dinner while tuning in. You have less control over the learning environment each of your participants occupies, but you can design sessions so they invite a constant return to engagement (minute to minute or week to week).

Model Student Digital Resources

Take advantage of the online training platform to demonstrate the tools and resources that your museum or site recommends for students. Many educators teach in online environments, and you may gain new inspiration in how to apply your digital resources to their students' learning by taking them through it. During the modeling exercise, invite feedback and ask for creative input into the best way to instruct teachers on how to use your institution's digital offerings. Elevate your expectations for chats, polls, and breakout rooms to support the generation of new ideas from teachers in your student-focused online experiences.

Sustained Programs

The second format can also be seen as a combination of different formats. The key here is to design opportunities to engage with the same teachers for an intensive or extended period of time. Investing your institution's expertise in this focused manner is mutually beneficial to you and the teachers who participate. Their work can become more and more reflective of your institution's strengths, and your institution's outreach to teachers can be built on authentic and meaningful expertise learned from their classroom implementation. Sustained programs can also form ties with schools, districts, and states that outlive the individuals who initially attended your programs.

At Mount Vernon, our sustained program models fall into two distinct categories. The first is programs that run at the same time annually and serve the same audience. These programs largely serve the teachers in our local area (although this is changing with the growth of digital programs) and are a chance for us to connect with the same teachers each year and welcome new ones "into the fold." The second type of sustained program is illustrated by the alumni cohort-building we do after our in-depth residential program. Because we put so many hours of training into a teacher in one short amount of time, we want to sustain our connection to that teacher for many years to come. So in addition to offering the program, we continue offering special connections and opportunities to these teachers, knowing they have had such intense training with us.

A sustained program is greater than the sum of its individual sessions. Built into the program design should be a structure to support cumulative growth in the participant and his or her connections to your institution. While not every participant will return the investment, those who do will become mission-advocates for your work in places out of your direct reach. Whether this relationship grows over a week, a year, or a decade, the benefits to your understanding of this audience and the resources exchanged will transform your work, making it more teacher centric.

Sustain Community Building with Unscheduled and Social Time

Multiday programs include shared mealtimes, roommates, theater outings, and early access to historic areas. These can build group cohesion and elevate learning opportunities for all involved. Informal conversations can provide some of the most memorable encounters for participants, scholars, and program planners. If interactions are encouraged beyond planned and formal sessions, you extend and strengthen your long-term relationship with many of the teachers.

Seek and Support Mission Advocates

When supporting teachers through multiple training sessions or extended series, you are forging a bond with these participants that extends beyond simple transference of your resources to their classroom. Be proactive about enhancing this relationship by inviting teachers to advocate for your institution beyond their classroom. Ask them to present resources to the colleagues in their school or district. Find opportunities for them to speak at a donor event, a board meeting, or a community outreach session about your institution's future—the voice of a supporting teacher can be invaluable. Representing your organization at local social studies and history instruction conferences provides networking and extended learning experiences for your teacher advocate and gives you a greater reach into the educator community via an authentic peer.

Build Teacher Leadership Skills

For sustained engagement with teachers, invite them to spend time learning and practicing their leadership skills. Create sessions that focus on advocacy skills, public speaking, and empowerment. Use content from your institution to identify historic figures they can teach their students about, as well as to inspire their practice. The teachers you invest in with leadership development skills take on leadership roles in their schools and communities. Your support of them in these areas improves your institution's connections to a greater network of educators. You can ask them to apply those leadership skills for the benefit of your institution by inviting them to author institutional content.

Key Elements to Strengthen Every PD Program

After you take stock of your program format options, put those options in dialogue with your target audience needs and your institutional culture, vision, and mission to ensure you have the right format for the work you want to do. If you believe you have the right format, it's time to start building the program. There are four key program elements that should be included in every program to ensure its effectiveness: *site experiences, historical focus, classroom application,* and *reflection.* Use these sections as a checklist to design the best possible professional development program, one that supports teachers in the classroom with the assets your institution brings to bear.

Site Experiences

If you take a look at your program design and see that it could easily be replicated in a hotel conference center or school district training room, then you are not maximizing the most powerful resource of your teacher professional development. Your site and collection are at the heart of connecting your institutional strengths with teacher needs. Historical places and authentic objects are critical for teachers' ability to foster critical thinking skills and empower their students to think like historians.

Integrating site and source experiences can be as simple as providing a tour of your space during the program, offering guided exploration, or highlighting objects from the collection. The key to making it effective is to build connections between the theme of your program and the experience teachers are having at your site and with your collection. This can be through participant-generated inquiry or by using a carefully crafted script. Either way, be sure you are using your site experience and object engagement time for constructive meaning-making that helps achieve the end objective of your program. Below are some possible site or source experiences to inspire integration into your program.

Explore During the Site Overview

Don't waste a site overview by starting and ending with basic orientation. Use the time you dedicate to orientation to connect your space with the goals of the site or exhibit, and invite the participants to see your spaces through historical, pedagogical, and skill-building perspectives. Let your site tell its story to them.

Site Exploration in Online Programs

Digital programs offer the lucky opportunity to engage participants who are attending from different locations. In addition to sharing your location online, you can also encourage critical thinking about historic sites by asking participants to analyze their own workspace, home, school, or neighborhood. These skills are both transferrable to historic sites and student learning. These spaces are more familiar to your participants but analyzing them takes the same skills as in a historic area or cultural site.

Model Student Tours

If a modeled student tour is part of your program for teachers, ensure that you are listening as much as sharing. Teachers are very skilled at bringing their students' perspectives to a learning activity, and can contribute to improving it. Pause at transition moments, invite sharing, and relinquish control at key points to explore with the teachers the strategies built into the tour. Conclude with prompted reflective time so they can process it from their perspective and through the lens of the students.

Collaborate with Other Sites

Establish your expectations with partner sites so teachers can expect a comparable experience in both places. If the culture and strategies at the two sites are distinct, show those differences. Take advantage of the contrast to extend the learning.

Offer VIP and Special Access Experiences

Designing behind-the-scenes and exclusive access heightens the excitement level for teacher participants. Maximize the "coolness" factor by making the museum practices and historical thinking skills visible. While you might not be able to offer this access to their students (in the classroom, online, or on-site), giving teachers these opportunities will help them see how historical thinking is part of our work process, just as it is for their students.

Offer Discrete and Focused Experiences

Providing self-guided or directed exhibit activities (like scavenger hunts or "See Think Wonder" routines) demonstrates pathways for new ways of teaching with primary sources. Having teams do the activities also allows for informal or directed collaboration between participants and contributes to the rewarding feeling that "your site" is now a place that belongs to them. This is a good goal for any site experience strategy; when teachers feel like your museum is their playground, you both win.

Historical Focus

The foundation of most museum-school partnerships is the content of the institution. Your institution's historical subject matter likely provides the most direct alignment with the school's curriculum; it may also be your funders' priorities and the most visible part of your institution's mission within the community. Use your content expertise as a cornerstone for the other program components to build on.

At historic sites and museums, historical content is sometimes over-looked or invisible because of its assumed relevance to teacher professional development. If your site interprets the history of a specific state or region, you and your teachers may just assume your programs will include that history. And yes, that's true, but as the strategies listed next suggest, being intentional about the focus you bring to your disciplinary expertise will strengthen the program. Nothing that is programmed to run on auto-pilot will soar.

Embrace a School View of Your Content

You bring excitement and enthusiasm to content, but don't jump to tangents and surprisingly unexpected directions your collection can take a student without first drawing the sharp lines between your content and the curricula that frame classroom instruction. Lean on the work a district or state has already done to align to your content, or identify how your content fits into standard-prioritized national or global events. If direct connections are lacking or tenuous, try connecting to district or state standards in historical thinking or essential questions.

Show Your History Work

Narrative history is powerful, but alone it can be limiting. If all you provide is your interpretation of history, you stop short of giving teachers ownership of your content. Give them the tools and inspiration to construct their lessons based on the source material and expertise you give them in training. Model and narrate the historical thinking process for those teachers less familiar with this approach. Take the time during content presentations to illustrate why your institution draws the conclusions it does and what sources it uses to construct its interpretations. Ideally, teachers will gain a strong historical story to tell, improved historical thinking skills, and practical inspiration on how to use sources, context, and inquiry to design a lesson for their students.

Prepare Your History Experts

Connecting teachers with curators, archivists, and other scholars grounds the historical content throughout a program. Outline expectations for your scholars beyond the content you would like them to share. Ensure they understand teachers' needs, have an engaging presence, demonstrate respect for the teaching profession, and are willing to make their historical work and sources visible. When I approach a new scholar for a teacher program, we start by talking about the educators they've valued in their life. If they've done teacher PD sessions before, I ask what they've learned from the teachers for whom they presented. I seek out their videos of presentations online to see how they integrate sources and make historical thinking visible. I talk frankly about the balance we expect between sharing their scholarship and sharing their process. Assess their skills and plan the program for their strengths. Will they be most effective in a panel, as a solo presenter, giving a tour, or fielding wide-ranging questions from your participants? Share the full program schedule with them to limit overlap with other sessions. Remind them that teachers are professionals with advanced degrees who bring their own expertise to each session.

Establish Content Goal Posts

Just as would a teacher, use bell ringers, ice breakers, and trivia games to gauge your participants' working knowledge throughout the program. Intermittent check-ins allow you to assess for new content acquisition before building upon those ideas. Low-tech tools, like sticky note voting, as well as online systems can do this both quickly and unobtrusively. Incorporating check-ins as a routine will make it feel familiar and nonthreatening.

History Content Is Traumatic

Teaching history well means covering topics that include human suffering and injustice. History is volatile and personal, and every time your program delves into the past you create potential routes to both joy and trauma for your participants. Recognize the power of the content you are presenting. Ensure you lead sessions that allow for individual responses and that those responses are all honored with respect. Whether using tools that evoke emotions, like dramatic interpretations, or relying on analytical data drawn from historical records, be ready to support your teachers in processing their own journey in response to the content you share. Be sure that there are check-ins with your teachers, especially when you have an external expert presenting. Coach the scholar in advance and let them know you or a facilitator will be pausing to check in on teachers through challenging and revealing content. When your program starts, ensure your teachers have a strong understanding of the physical space and the culture of learning that supports their access to other rooms as needed and encourages them to have and voice responses that diverge from the interpretation your institution presents.

Classroom Application

Professional development offerings at historic sites and museums are distinctly different from sessions offered by schools and districts, but they must be equally effective in supporting classroom application. While the assets you offer teachers in these trainings can be exciting and inspiring, they must also be useful. If you want to extend your institution's mission into the classroom by supporting teachers, the training you offer must provide the tools to do that. Also, embrace the humility that, as informal educators working outside the classroom, you and your colleagues may not know the best ways to apply your resources to the classroom environment.

Assumed in the suggestions that follow is that your program will not just tell, but also show how to take your resources and bring them into the classroom or guided tours. Whether this is done by highlighting preexisting resources or cocreating them with participants, a successful professional development program will be more effective if you model classroom application.

Honor Teacher Expertise in Program Development

In order to integrate meaningful classroom application into your programming, it is vital to involve teachers, librarians, and/or discipline specialists in your planning and execution. This involvement can be in the form of advisory boards at the macro scale or teacher-led presentations at the micro level. Either way (or both ways!) will help you maintain authentic and realistic examples of applying your resources to classroom instruction.

Embrace the "Thinking Like a Historian" Approach

Teaching history can no longer be summed up as knowledge of events and dates. The benefits of history instruction to student learning is practice and mastery of the historical thinking process. Inquiry, source analysis, and perspective-taking are vital skills for critical-thinking students. Public historians at your institution are in the business of asking questions, drawing conclusions from evidence, and interpreting history from a point of view. In sharing these museum techniques, you provide a valuable and real-world model for teachers.

Recognize the Diversity of Teaching Environments

Participants in your program may come from schools that represent a wide variety of grade levels, geographic regions, cultural backgrounds, economic landscapes, and accessibility considerations. Your sessions cannot possibly prepare for every teacher's unique classroom, but you can combat the one-size-fits-all resource assumption. Acknowledge classroom differences and build in time for guidance or brainstorming to create versions personalized for individual classrooms.

Offer Recommendations, Troubleshooting Tips, and Next Steps

To support classroom application, continue to help teachers after your program ends. You and your institution should be considered resources to support the integration of your sources and strategies into their student learning plans. It is surely unrealistic to offer one-on-one coaching to every teacher after the program is over, but you can show that you are invested in their success by preparing materials that anticipate stumbling blocks or suggest additional reading. This demonstrates your support in the long run, and with that safety net, they are more likely to take risks and try new techniques included in your training. When a teacher does reach out for assistance afterward, it's a great opportunity to build a more sustained relationship with that teacher and his or her school and district.

Reflection

Although most often cut and seen as a "nice-to-have" instead of a "need-to-have," research has shown that reflection is one of the most critical components in a teacher professional development session if your expectation is for participants to transfer your work to their practice. The next time you find yourself cutting out reflection time for the sake of a content expert or how-to session, think about all that you lose if that material never makes it to the students because the teacher didn't have the time to reflect on its value and connections.

Integrating reflection is more than adding longer breaks to your program (although those are good, too). As the program designer, you can activate the reflective practice and make it visible in a way that gives the participant control over it and makes it more effective.

Provide Prompts, Methods, and Time for Self-Reflection

While helpful for some, undirected self-reflection can cause other participants to become frustrated or roll their eyes. As the program designer, you can create the expectation for regular reflection within the program structure; prompts between sessions and anticipated, built-in methods, like journaling or concept mapping, all support meaningful self-reflection. Whichever method you choose, make it clear to participants that the purpose is to clarify their own thinking and that they won't be expected to share.

Create Opportunities for Community Reflection

Divulging individual reflections, especially if the exercise asks for vulnerability, can be disruptive to the process; however, if an activity is clearly designed for group reflection, it can break down barriers between the participants and collectively connect participants to your mission. Conducting a social truth exercise, answering questions by voting with your feet, or launching a hypothetical shopping trip for instructional tools to bring back to the classroom serve these dual goals.

Learning History Is Personal

Providing reflective activities that engage teachers in identity work is memorable and powerful. By working to acknowledge their own relationship to the content at your institution, they will better prepare themselves to teach students with your resources. They will also be able to support students who are working to understand their own relationship to history.

Use the Lens of School and District Expectations

Invite participants to recall and reflect on their school requirements during your program. Help them chart a realistic path from your materials to their existing expectations. Perhaps their district has go-to thinking routines that align nicely with the inquiry and sources your session addressed. This practice can tether the exciting new ideas they have to actionable standards and expectations for their classrooms. It can also make it easier for them to share what they've learned with their colleagues.

Integrate Ritual and Ceremony

Building into your program ceremonial or ritual components can invite shared reflection, emotion, and intentional goal-setting. Graduation ceremonies and daily pair-and-share rituals give shape to the instruction. Land acknowledgment statements and memorialization ceremonies formally recognize the connections participants have to the past. Authoring a "statement of intent" or a letter to your future self during a program can help ground individual goals that, once made tangible, are easier to return to afterward.

Conclusion

Creating a teacher professional development program for a history museum or historic site can be a powerful and meaningful experience for both the institution and the teachers served. Finding the right balance of history instruction, classroom application, and reflection that lives authentically within your mission and site takes time and intention. The elements in this article are not comprehensive but are offered to suggest the breadth of what can be achieved. Consulting this practical list can help shape your program's format and components to match your institution's assets in the best way to serve the teachers in your communities. If revising an existing program, define what is already great about it while determining ways to innovate and strengthen it.

Teachers deserve our institutional respect, for without them we would be limited in achieving our educational missions. Our museums can be champions for educators and, with these programs, can demonstrate our commitment to their professional achievements and recognize the important civic duty they've embraced by educating the leaders of our future. And because it didn't fit in anywhere else, one last tip for successful teacher program professional development: feed them well. Invest in the "good" food spread that comes with the fancy drinks whenever feasible. It will be worth it.

Program schedules for in-person and virtual, weeklong and weekend, and endless other program permutations can be found at teacherinsites.org. You'll find ideas for sessions and also see how to balance time between content, pedagogy, and networking.

8

Recruitment and Selection

Melanie Bowyer and Jacqueline Langholtz

The Monticello Teacher Institute (MTI) is an immersive professional development program that provides social studies teachers with the opportunity to research and study at Monticello and the Jefferson Library in Charlottesville, Virginia. Learn more at monticello.org/mti.

In 2014, professional development for teachers at Monticello transformed from a program that had served two to three teachers per summer with a research focus to one that served around thirty each summer and emphasized collaborative learning. The expansion of the program necessitated a thoughtful approach and a redesign of our recruiting and selection processes. By revisiting our program's goals, we developed an integrative approach to selecting and recruiting teachers to build the most successful cohorts possible.

An Unvarnished Internal Look and Recruiting for Diversity

A critical component of strengthening our program through recruitment is engaging a more diverse network of educators. We understand that a former plantation where men, women, and children were once enslaved based on their race means that we have extra work to do to convince black and brown educators that they are welcome and valued there. These historical disincentives are powerful barriers, and it is the responsibility of staff at historic sites like Monticello to remove them. Including a commitment to teaching complex and contested history and to welcoming diverse perspectives is a good start.

We know that word of mouth is a powerful recruitment tool; so, too, is asking for support from your network. One thing we've done to increase racial diversity in our applicant pool is to tell our MTI alumni that we need their help and welcome their recommendations. Referrals have helped build diversity within the program. But we know we need to do more, including addressing a diversity gap within our own team. While lack of diversity is a problem that is not unique to Monticello, our staff consistently works toward correcting this crucial and ongoing issue.

Teachers Recruiting Teachers: Creating a Teacher Ambassador Corps

For diversity and beyond, one of the most effective ways we have found to promote MTI is by intentional word of mouth. We designed a program with the goal that our participants will become ambassadors for us throughout the country. As such, they present about their work to colleagues at school, regional, or state gatherings. They have represented Monticello in exhibitor halls at education conferences to specifically answer their peers' questions about professional development at Monticello.

In conceiving our goals for increasing teacher engagement with Monticello, we created a Pyramid of Teacher Engagement (see figure 8.1) to help us identify avenues and areas of opportunity. If we first encountered a teacher at a conference presentation, perhaps we could convince that teacher to plan an in-person or virtual field trip to Monticello, use a lesson from our website, or apply to the MTI. While there is no single right path to engagement, and a teacher won't necessarily start on the lowest level or progress in the exact order as listed, the Pyramid of Teacher Engagement helped us define the ultimate goal for ourselves: enlisting and empowering an ambassador corps of teacher-advocates to help us promote, refine, and grow all our educational initiatives. The goal, with every opportunity, was to move teachers up the pyramid. We've since added an additional level of engagement with the creation of a Teacher Advisory Group, an invited set of alumni who formally advise our education team and Monticello as a whole on initiatives related to teacher and student outreach.

This advocacy work on the part of "teacher ambassadors" helped launch MTI in an entirely new way. We saw more than a 150 percent increase in applications to MTI, leading to the need for a more competitive selection process. Traffic to our digital classroom website increased from about 86,000 in 2011 to well over 300,000 by 2015. Similarly, our social media sites quickly gained new followers as our staff and teacher alumni interacted with more than 1,500 educators at various conferences across the country, reaching ten states in 2016 alone. Ambassadors also help promote and share our posts on social media; today, our public Teach

Pyramid of teacher engagement

Figure 8.1.   Teacher Engagement Pyramid. Courtesy of Monticello, Thomas Jefferson Foundation.

Monticello Facebook account has nearly 1,800 followers and Twitter's @teachmonticello has more than 2,200. A Facebook group started by a Monticello ambassador, the Monticello Teacher's Institute Alumni group, has more than one hundred members and is a way for the alumni network to continue its peer-to-peer learning and mutual support via digital means.

How You Talk about Your Program

Provide a Clear Description of the Program

Review anything that describes your program, including printed materials and web text. If you were someone with no prior knowledge of the program, the site, or TPD in general, would the available information speak for itself, or would you have only a partial or incomplete understanding of the opportunity? Since confusion about the experience can present barriers and complications to applications, stay ahead of those by continually reviewing your materials with fresh eyes and ensuring that any assumptions or ambiguities are addressed.

With this goal in mind, we reviewed MTI's website from the perspective of a person with no prior knowledge of the program, or of Monticello itself, compared it with the websites of similar institutes, and made some improvements. Among those were adding a short, bulleted list outlining:

- program activities
- a description of the application process
- who was eligible to apply and what the selection process involved
- information about funding and certificates of completion
- acknowledgment of accessibility needs

A video of teacher testimonials was added to bring educators' voices forward, and photos on the page show racial diversity to clearly message our wish to be inclusive and welcoming to all. These changes, paired with the heading on the top of the application stating our goal to "bring together a diverse group of teachers who are excited to work together to advance history education in classrooms across America," significantly altered how we presented the program to others, and what we asked of them in return.

State Your Program's Values

The ambassador program provided the spark to get teachers interested in and aware of MTI. Concurrently, we had to think about how we described the program in print and online. This may sound obvious, but the most important reminders are these: Remember your program's goals in all your communications. Ensure you're clearly messaging your institutional values and that this alignment—because it is at the core of everything you do—is evident in everything from flyers to videos to social media posts

We revised our programs goals in 2017 after completing the Q-Methodology evaluation the summer prior. This prompted us to take a step back and reframe for ourselves first what the program was about. We settled upon wanting to bolster teachers' historical thinking skills, presenting a nuanced and complex view of history, demonstrating relevance of our site's history and resources, and creating a collaborative program that would be refreshing to teachers and build connections between educators and our institution. See our full list at teacherinsites.org.

to your application. To accomplish this, we frequently state "Monticello is committed to the study and teaching of difficult history." In the application, we asked teachers to "Give a specific example of how you approach a challenging topic (i.e., race, religion, gender, politics) with your students." In adding this question, we sought to signal our intent to tackle difficult, sensitive, and oftentimes uncomfortable subject matter while providing an avenue for teachers to tell us about their teaching style and comfort levels. Our values-based question may not be *your* values-based question; yours will be unique to your program's goals and your internal culture. We recommend you take the time to wrestle with this question and prototype it until it achieves what you want it to. Your values-based question is also a statement. What does yours say about you?

Designing an Application with Purpose

By 2016, we were receiving well over one hundred applications for roughly thirty spots in our weeklong summer institute. That constituted a "good problem." But the responses we were getting to our application questions weren't telling us everything we wanted to know about our applicants—we still felt that the selection process was a bit of a guessing game. To address this, we decided the first step in the improvement process was to take a critical look at our application. Rather than open-ended questions that garnered generic answers—such as "State your interest in participating in this opportunity"—we refined and narrowed our questions to elicit answers that better aligned with the traits we were hoping to find in ideal candidates. We also amended or added questions to ensure the application itself was more mission-aligned and that it clearly indicated our intent to tackle complex history, embrace complexities, integrate new technologies, and invite diverse perspectives. In other words, we weren't looking for people who saw only a one-dimensional Jefferson; we wanted to promote peer-to-peer learning and a collaborative environment. Over the next few years, the application questions grew, changed, and gained greater focus. We believe these changes made a significant impact on the program by giving applicants greater insight into its goals and expectations while giving us more information about our applicant pool.

Include Prompts That Welcome Creative Responses

Since not all schools with high levels of need are classified as Title 1, we added an optional question inviting applicants to "provide any additional information about your school's community, student body, or mission that you would like us to know." Answers to this question often gave us much more valuable insight into student demographics and school culture than a Title 1 designation ever could. The question gave the teacher an opportunity to speak to their students' unique needs and interests. That one change was so simple, and so powerful!

To help teachers think beyond the traditional lesson plan as a final product, we asked applicants to "take a look through classroom.monti cello.org. What sources appeal to you the most? Based on your on-site research, what's a resource (e.g., activities, videos, reading sets) that you would like to contribute to the site? Feel free to get creative!" To support our program's goal of modeling and practicing historical thinking strategies—as opposed to passively consuming content —applicants were told that "MTI gives teachers a chance to step into the role of historian and engage in research in order to create new resources for students." Teachers were then asked to provide a description of how their proposed research focus used historical thinking. Answers to this question not only provided insight into a teacher's proposed research focus, but also gave us a sense of their conception of what it means to "do history."

We signaled that the MTI has a "collaborative, hands-on environment where participants work closely with their peers," and asked, "How do you hope to contribute to the group's experience?" Related to the idea of collaboration and building a community of practice, we also added an application question with a declarative statement: "Each MTI participant makes a commitment to become a Monticello ambassador." Along with this, we asked applicants to select the ways in which they would be willing to share their knowledge and experience with other educators and students after the institute ended. For ambassador work with fellow educators, options included recommending a colleague for the MTI, arranging a digital field trip of professional development, distributing materials, etc. For ambassador work with students, we asked whether applicants would rather have their students participate in an electronic field trip, complete a responsive art or writing project to share with Monticello, or come on a Monticello field trip. For each population, we asked applicants to tell us which options they found most exciting, as well as which seemed most challenging. This seeded the idea that this experience was not self-contained and gave us a sense of a teacher's interest in the extension work that our program ambassadors engage in.

In the process of both designing and reviewing applications, a program must also determine who it can and wants to serve. New teachers? Veteran teachers? Local or far-flung? We have intentionally recruited for geographic diversity in order to both fuel our ambassadorships and find a mix of newer and more experienced teachers. The result is mentorship opportunities and infusions of new approaches and ideas when developing classroom resources. When assessing questions about historical thinking and teaching complex topics, we do not simply select teachers who appear to have mastered these skills; we select those who are open to a collaborative conversation and are looking for support.

Aligning the Selection Process with Values: Using a Rubric to Guide Application Review and Selection

The next step in the process was the creation of a rubric to aid in application selection. A four-person staff review panel and an inevitably short window to review applications necessitated extra attention to consistency and fairness across the application review process. Taking a cue from the formal education field, we developed a twelve-point rubric (see table 8.1) to rate applicants based on traits and criteria we were looking for in an ideal participant. Aligning the rubric with the questions we asked in the application allowed us to make more consistent decisions as a team, while also helping us notice patterns within our applicant pool that could identify needed changes in messaging, expectations, or planning.

While we wholeheartedly recommend using a rubric to guide your application review and selection process, keep in mind that any rubric you use should be specifically aligned to your program's mission and goals. Rubrics are not a "one size fits all" proposition, so take the time to draft a tool that will be uniquely suited to your site, your program, and your needs. We recommend circulating it for internal review and edits before it is adopted for use, and taking time after each application process to tweak the design for future years, if necessary. Remember, the goal is constant improvement!

The four themes our rubric measured were "Teaching Historical Thinking," "Collaborative Contributions," "Proposed Research Focus," and "Ambassador Potential." Each of these aligned with the program's central goals and helped us remain focused and impartial when reviewing applications. In crafting the rubric's criteria, we were specific in our examples and thoughtful in our word choices. The rubric had a structure and concepts that could be useful to other selection committees but were specifically tailored to our site and program. Low scores helped us make initial cuts to the applicant pool. The winnowing continued from there, with selection committee members typically bringing their 7s or 8s and forward for consideration. Additional notes fields included grade level, geographic location, preferred session, Title 1 designation, and "other," which aided the sorting process.

Once you devote many hours to reviewing applications, remember to keep all those notes you made! Our team repeatedly found that our notes came in handy when we received unexpected cancellations and the opportunity to pull an applicant off the waiting list, or when we needed to quickly refresh our memory on why an applicant was or was not

Table 8.1. Monticello Teacher Institute Application Rubric, 2020

Theme	3 Points	2 Points	1 Point	0 Points
Teaching Historical Thinking (including multiple perspectives, teaching difficult history, etc.)	Response articulates specific desire to gain experience in and/or concrete past experience with at least TWO of the following: enhancing skills related to historical thinking strategies; interest in tackling contemporary or sensitive subjects through a historical lens; an "ah-ha" moment or paradigm shift; and interest in developing new resources for teaching the relevance of Jefferson's ideas/legacy today.	Response articulates specific desire to gain experience in and/or concrete past experience with at least ONE of the following: enhancing skills related to historical thinking strategies; interest in tackling contemporary or sensitive subjects through a "aha" moment or paradigm shift; and interest in developing new resources for teaching the relevance of Jefferson's ideas/legacy today.	Response shows general awareness or interest in learning more about relevant historical themes related to Thomas Jefferson and/or Monticello and the importance of teaching them in today's classrooms.	Response is incomplete, unrelated, includes factual inaccuracies, or perpetuates harmful stereotypes.
Collaborative Contributions	Answer includes at least one positive, concrete example of engaging in collaborative, peer-to-peer learning; in working as part of a diverse team; or of describing a product that was the result of a collaborative team effort.	Answer articulates a clearly stated desire to meet new people, learn from others, and/or participating in group activities with peers.	Answer expresses a general interest in participating in group or cohort professional development experience.	Response is incomplete, unrelated, includes factual inaccuracies, or perpetuates harmful stereotypes.

Proposed Research Focus	Proposed topic is appropriately narrow and demonstrates evidence of historical thinking, innovative teaching strategies, contemporary and Monticello relevance, strong classroom connections, and originality.	Proposed topic demonstrates clear classroom connections and relevancy to key historic or contemporary themes related to Monticello.	Proposed topic is too broad, repeats lesson plans or resources already available without adding a new idea, teaching strategy, or perspective.	Response is incomplete, unrelated, includes factual inaccuracies, or perpetuates harmful stereotypes.
Ambassador Potential	Applicant shows enthusiasm for sharing their MTI experiences, selecting four or more ways to share with both teachers and students, and may offer additional original ideas that align with MTI outcomes.	Applicant selected three or more concrete examples of how they would share MTI experiences with both teachers and students.	Applicant selected few or limited ways to share their MTI experiences and/or only focuses on students rather than their peers.	Response is incomplete, unrelated, includes factual inaccuracies, or perpetuates harmful stereotypes.

Source: Courtesy of Monticello, Thomas Jefferson Foundation.

admitted to the program in the past. Keeping these completed rubrics accessible and appropriately archived can also help you identify and track changing patterns in your applicant pool. Notice that you never get applications from Oklahoma? Maybe it's time to do some targeted outreach. Seem like 80% of applicants request the same session? Could be a good idea to review your scheduling approach.

What We Learned (and Are Still Learning!)

Our growth with the MTI has happened in fits and starts. At times, it felt downright messy. In reflecting back on the program's history, we are reminded that the improvement process is iterative, reflective, and often nonlinear. Some years we focused on enriching the program activities or application, while others were spent overhauling our catering model. One positive change usually inspired or prompted another. And every time we attended a workshop and admired something a museum peer or member of our local community was doing, we looked for a way to integrate it into our model. We made mistakes along the way, but we made every effort to turn those into teachable moments for ourselves.

In reflecting back on the MTI's evolution, we are encouraged by the increase in the numbers of teachers and students served and the ways we strived to improve the program in terms of content, practice, and diversity. We are also struck by the opportunities for improvement and—most importantly—the extent to which we must acknowledge that we still have room to grow. Happily, this opportunity to reflect on our process has sparked a renewed commitment to revisit many of these same goals of recruitment and engagement with a reminder to continually challenge ourselves to invite more diverse perspectives and seek stakeholder input. We hope that engaging in this reflective process will improve the support we give teachers and positively impact all who participate in these programs in the future, both at Monticello and at other historic sites.

8.5

A Teacher's Perspective

Karen Richey

Karen Richey teaches middle school history and social science at Toby Johnson Middle School in Elk Grove, California. Karen firmly believes that professional development that takes place at historic sites and museums not only enriches the practice of the teachers who participate but also creates national networks that support and sustain teachers in unexpected ways.

I began teaching in 1996. For the first half of my career, I lacked knowledge of professional development opportunities beyond what was offered at the district or state level. In 2009, my district offered teachers the opportunity to earn a master's degree in history partially funded by a Teaching American History grant. The timing was not optimal, but the opportunity was too good to pass up. So with the support of my family, I became a graduate student at age thirty-nine.

At the end of one class, the professor gently scolded us about not taking advantage of national workshop opportunities. I was teaching full time, taking full-time graduate school units at night, and caring for an infant and a four-year-old at home. When would I have time to attend more professional development, especially if it required travel? Dr. Burke's comments stuck with me, though, and I applied to a Gilder Lehrman seminar for the summer of 2011. The seminar greatly shaped my thesis project. Thanks to that experience, I began to see myself as part of an intellectual community of teacher-historians, and I was absolutely hooked on high-quality professional development that focused on primary sources and the power of place.

The National Endowment for the Humanities Landmarks workshop hosted by Ford's Theatre in Washington, DC, during the summer of 2015 is a perfect example of what I mean. Would I like a chance to meet and learn from "rock star" historians such as Martha Hodes, Kenneth Foote, and Terry Alford? Yes, please! How about the opportunity to visit historic sites including Ford's Theatre, the Peterson House, Frederick Douglass's home, Howard University, and the Surratt House in Maryland? Sign me up! Would I benefit from time to connect with colleagues from around the nation and reflect on our learning and its implications for our classrooms? I'll say! Let me pack my bags!

Ford's Theatre's staff ensured that teachers had time throughout the workshop to process what we learned and discuss its implementation in our classrooms. My eighth-grade American history course spans events from Revolution to Reconstruction, but my students often struggle to connect with events that happened both long ago and far away. The Gold Rush is the only time California enters our textbook's narrative in any substantial way. Martha Hodes's research from *Mourning Lincoln* and resources from Ford's Remembering Lincoln website inspired me to create a lesson that focused on how different Californians reacted to the news of Abraham Lincoln's assassination. David McKenzie at Ford's worked with me to format my lesson for the Remembering Lincoln site, where it can still be accessed as a resource for other teachers.

I tell my students that the summer workshops I attend are camp for history nerds. Teachers share intense learning experiences and form deep and lasting connections. Caitlin Goodwin was one of the colleagues I connected with at Ford's Theatre. We both teach middle school history, on opposite sides of the country—New York and California. When Caitlin and I roomed together during the workshop, we spent countless hours discussing the content of the workshop and teaching in general. We kept in touch, and two summers later, she encouraged me to apply to Ford's Oratory Fellowship Program, where teachers study the art of effective oratory. I tried to explain to Caitlin why the oratory program was not for me. I sat in the front row of my college classes so that I would have the courage to speak without everyone turning to look at me. Yes, I am a teacher and speak in front of students all day, but applying to become an oratory fellow meant making a commitment to work toward excellence in a skill that terrified me. Caitlin's belief in me gave me the courage to be braver than I would have been on my own. I applied to be an oratory fellow. I felt both terrified and thrilled when I was notified of my acceptance into the program.

Oratory fellows learn the four core principles of Ford's Oratory Fellowship Program: rhetorical triangle, podium points, warm and cool feedback, and an actor's approach to connecting to texts. Fellows work closely with a Ford's Theatre teaching artist to incorporate the core oratory principles in their unique classroom environment. The learning curve was steep. I often felt overwhelmed and worried that I would not be able to succeed during my first year as a fellow. Monthly Zoom meetings were a lifeline. The kind and patient mentoring of Ford's staff and the more experienced fellows gave me the support I needed to grow into the program.

I recently completed my fourth year as an oratory fellow with Ford's Theatre and served as their Teacher in Residence during the summer of 2019. The Fellows Retreat held at the end of my residency was the last time we all gathered in person. One of the activities we participated in used pins and yarn on a map of the US to create a visual representation of our connections. All the threads led to Washington, DC, of course, but many fellows have visited one another's homes as well. Caitlin has been to my house, and I hope to visit her in New York someday. The threads connecting us as fellows have held strong throughout the pandemic as our monthly Zoom meetings provide a space for us to offer one another support and inspire ideas.

This summer, I will travel to Iceland as a Fulbright scholar with a group of K–8 educators. My Fulbright project's focus on Icelandic sagas and the importance of storytelling as a form of history comes directly from my work with Ford's Oratory Fellowship Program. I look forward to sharing what I learn in Iceland with the other fellows, as I know that their thoughtful feedback will strengthen my project.

9

Teacher-Created Projects

Classroom and Museum Resources

Krystal Rose

This chapter explores options for teacher-created products at site-based teacher professional development (TPD) programs through the experiences of the education team at Mystic Seaport Museum. After examining the qualities of different teacher-created products and approaches, we share other critical considerations for planning and hosting product-creation TPD.

In 2010, Mystic Seaport Museum, a 19-acre maritime museum, village, and shipyard in Mystic, Connecticut, set out to create an innovative online platform for educators and students. The project team and consultants felt it imperative to involve educators during every step of the process, especially in the research and development phase. As a result, the participating education professionals made it clear what they wanted out of the project: to stay involved, use the collections, and author and create the resources of the online platform. Teachers know the classroom and their students better than anyone; cocreating resources is a beneficial conduit for bringing museum content into their curriculum.

Giving teachers a chance to author and create resources became the driving force behind our professional development opportunities. We hoped that by involving teachers in a participatory model, they would become invested in the resources, use and share them in their schools, and become ambassadors for the museum. Using the data and ideas from four years of research, which included more than fifty focus groups, the museum's education team began an initiative of inviting K–12 educators into the library, vaults, exhibits, and grounds, with the hopes of starting a new type of educator collaboration for the museum. The participants worked with staff members and other educators to learn, create, and, in many cases, reignite the spark that inspired them to teach in the first place. Nina Simon's work in *The Participatory Museum* is the inspiration for much of this participatory programming. According to Simon,

> Supporting participation means trusting visitors' abilities as creators, remixers, and redistributors of content. It means being open to the possibility that a project can grow and change post-launch beyond the institution's original intent. Participatory projects make relationships among staff members, visitors, community participants, and stakeholders more fluid and equitable. They open up new ways for diverse people to express themselves and engage with institutional practice.[1]

With Simon's words in mind, the museum experimented with various models of professional development in which teachers were the creators of museum resources. The resources themselves have taken multiple forms over the years, with the most successful types serving as anchors of the museum's website, Mystic Seaport for Educators (MSE). Our objectives for each program include connecting educators to museum resources, developing teacher-made products connected to the Common Core State Standards Initiative, and providing space for teachers to spend time together.

Here, we offer two approaches to teacher-created products and their associated programs as case studies:

- The *collections-based online resources* case study looks at two resource-creation models for the MSE website: the *Summer Fellows* model and the *Teacher-Curator Partnership* model. Teachers work with museum staff to develop website features for the MSE website in both of these models. The resources include artifact articles, living documents, story maps, interviews, and resource sets. The Summer Fellows model allows for a very flexible schedule and incorporates instructional classes, brainstorming sessions, and a focus on teacher-to-teacher camaraderie and collaboration. The Teacher-Curator Partnership model is a more individualized program, focusing on the relationship between teacher and curator and with a concentration on a specific topic, usually in line with an exhibit.
- The *Digital Hallway* approach will look at shorter teacher programs (three days or less) that focus on more typical teacher-created resources, like lesson plans and their evolution to a new platform, demonstrating how our thinking around traditional lesson plans changed.

Determining the Desired Product

In the early stages of developing the MSE website, museum staff worked with educators and web developers to figure out the best way to bring the museum collections to life online. The early iterations of what eventually became the signature components of the website started as vague research papers submitted by educators. Museum staff and web developers deconstructed and rearranged the content, trying to find the perfect combination of compelling content, the right length of text, connections to standards, ideas for the classroom, and high-quality imagery for student analysis. Throughout the process, we shared materials and drafts with educators and incorporated their feedback until the resource styles landed at a place with the right mix of information that educators and students desired. Before involving any educators in a formal professional development to produce materials, staff created templates and examples for each resource type. The templates and examples would prove essential tools in successfully creating programs where teachers develop quality resources. With the components in place, we were ready to try out various models for creating content with educators.

Cocreating Collections-Based Online Resources: The Summer Fellows Model

The Summer Fellows model was the first to test developing teacher-created products, an experiment backed by funding that allowed for several years of testing, tweaking, and creating. This model stemmed from the idea that teachers wanted to do authentic research, spend time with other educators, create non-lesson plan materials, and publish work on the MSE website. The guidelines for this program were very flexible, based on teacher feedback and needs. Teachers applied to the program and received a modest stipend upon project completion. At the beginning of the summer, five to ten teachers met for several days of orientation workshops, including collections tours with curators, writing workshops, research tutorials, and brainstorming sessions with staff and the other participants. Education staff also spent time carefully instructing teachers on how to use the templates to build their classroom resources. With the templates for artifact articles, living documents, and active maps in hand, teachers now worked to fill in the content and connect to standards by creating complementary ideas for use in the classroom. Initial subject matter selection was culled by museum staff based on teacher interest and standards connections. These lists of objects and documents were presented to the teachers during orientation for consideration and selection. One high school history teacher participant, Tina O'Brien from Providence, Rhode Island, remarked, "My favorite part of the program was

HOW TO CREATE ARTIFACT ARTICLES

BUT WAIT!

FIRST THING'S FIRST:

WHAT IS AN ARTIFACT ARTICLE?!

Artifact Articles (AAs) are short (2-3 paragraphs) pages which pertain to 1 object, and help to tell a greater story, and provide important contextual information about the object.
This will be initially created in a word document.

ARTIFACT ARTICLES ARE COMPRISED OF THE FOLLOWING SECTIONS:

- Artifact Stats (Record Info)
- Artifact Article Narrative
- Linked Information

- Questions For Deeper Thought
- Tags
- Ideas for Classroom Use
- Related Items From the Collection

- Related Resources
- Suggested Readings
- Bibliography
- Related Websites

Cool, but how do I make one?

Easy!

STEPS FOR CREATING AN ARTIFACT ARTICLE:

1. Pick an artifact that you would like to create an Artifact Article around.

2. *ARTIFACT STATS* -- Find the following information either on the collections website, or if not, ask Laura or Krystal to access through the MIMSY database:
   - Accession number
   - Object name
   - Object date
   - Maker (put unknown if unknown)
   - Associated Place
   - Measurements
   - Materials
   - Note if an image has been created – if not, please let Laura know so that we can create a work order for photo lab.

3. *ARTIFACT ARTICLE NARRATIVE* -- Conduct all necessary research in order to "tell the story" of not only this artifact, but also the context in which this object should be viewed in. For example, see "Azorean Whaling" (1965.889.1) at the end of this packet. You may want to figure out:
   - Any significance to people or places if it's a photograph, painting, print, etc
   - What is happening in the image if it's a photograph or painting or print
   - How the artifact was used if it's a tool or common object
   - Anything about the maker or creator
   - What is the over-arching story that this object helps to tell more about?

TIP: THINK OF WHICH RESOURCE SET THIS MAY LIVE IN. PLEASE REFER TO "RESOURCE SET" PAGE FOR A LIST OF CURRENT AND PROPOSED RESOURCE SETS

Figure 9.1. Template for Artifact Articles, created by Laura Nadelberg in 2014. Courtesy of Mystic Seaport Museum

the ability for each fellow to pick a piece that 'spoke' to us. I originally imagined myself choosing an object to research, but transcribing a journal became a much more inspiring spark."[2] The objects and documents selected by teachers had no particular theme.

Once teachers selected two objects or documents to work with, they collaborated with staff members for guidance in their research, making their schedules and visiting our library as needed. Halfway through the summer, the teachers submitted drafts for feedback. The cohort met again at the end of the summer to present their research and turn in their projects. Projects were reviewed again by staff, and some were eventually put online.

The Teacher-Curator Partnership Model

Our Teacher-Curator Partnership model is a more individualized program aligned with a current exhibition, project, or grant and involves fewer teachers. In this far more successful model, teachers collaborate directly with subject matter experts to create online resources. Like the Summer Fellows model, the Teacher-Curator Partnership focuses on a teacher doing research on flexible time, working with designated staff and experts, developing materials, and receiving a stipend. The model differs in that only one teacher is assigned to a given exhibit or project and a more formal relationship is nurtured between the teacher and the exhibit team. The teacher is involved in the exhibit design process almost from the beginning, which allows them to participate in the behind-the-scenes aspects of museum work. Once the curator selects objects and documents for the show, the teacher chooses items from the curator's selection to expand on for the website. Using the templates created for the Summer Fellows model, the educator creates materials for the MSE website that pull exclusively from the new exhibit. The curator is an active participant and offers guidance, expert advice, proofreading, and whatever is needed to get the materials into their final format, which makes it much easier for the website staff to get the final products onto the site. This model also involves the teacher in planning and executing a professional development session to promote the materials. O'Brien, who also participated in the Summer Fellows program, noted,

> I believe what worked well was the ability to build a teacher resource set based on an actual exhibit, so the inspiration to make the website real and relevant was crucial in my curriculum design . . . Mirelle [the curator] was available to proofread my artifact articles to check for historical accuracy . . . this experience was unlike any other professional development I have done because for the first time I was treated like a professional.[3]

The Mystic Seaport Museum has completed three successful iterations of this approach, resulting in resource sets on the MSE website about the *Sailor Made, Mary Mattingly's Open Ocean, Figureheads,* and *Sea as Muse* exhibits, funded by the Henry Luce Foundation.

Challenges and Rewards of Making Online Resources with Educators

Cocreating classroom resources with educators comes with challenges, which led us to morph the Summer Fellows program into the Teacher-Curator Partnership program. At the end of each Summer Fellows session, ten to twenty projects were submitted for publication on the website. While teachers had staff to guide them, the staff person was not always an expert in the content chosen by the teacher. With only two staff members—who also had other responsibilities—it was challenging to edit the pieces, check for accuracy, photograph objects, scan documents, and do the intricate work of entering and uploading the materials to the website. As the years went on, the backlog of teacher materials grew. It is also worth noting that not all teachers are used to writing and research-ing to the level of quality required for publication by the museum. How much rewriting and editing should museum staff do before losing the teacher's voice? About a quarter of the teacher products did not make it to the website in the Summer Fellows model.

When shifting to the Teacher-Curator Partnership model, we noted some key strengths of the Summer Fellows model that we wanted to carry forward. Teachers enjoyed learning from one another and spending time doing things important to them, like archival research. They created valuable materials and developed a sense of ownership and pride in the museum and its online resources. Teachers who participated in the pro-gram also served as ambassadors for the museum, sharing and presenting their materials back at school and in their districts, bringing awareness to the museum's mission and collections. The program's evolution into the Teacher-Curator Partnership model also solved the editorial challenges of writing and editing projects by increasing staff support directly available to the teachers. The refined process has led to a lower quantity of higher quality online classroom resources.

The Digital Hallway: Lesson Plans Get a Makeover

For years, Mystic Seaport Museum, like many other institutions, collected lesson plans from participants in professional development programs, in-cluding the Connecticut Teachers of the Year (CT TOY) program, a three-day TPD. The CT TOY program offered teachers the opportunity to go behind the scenes at our site, meet experts and other staff members, participate in hands-on activities (climbing the rigging is a favorite), spend time with like-minded educators, and create something for the museum. For the first few years of the program, that "something" was always a generic lesson plan, completed by the teacher during the program and shared on the MSE site. At the end of the first year, we received lesson plans from all the teachers. However, the number of submitted lesson plans dwindled over the years, and one summer we received no lesson plans at all.

The following year, we happened to be participating in the Q-Methodology evaluation described in chapter 5 of this book. While working with the project researchers, we learned some surprising information about lesson plans.

> It turns out, contrary to what many people think, very few teachers write out formal lesson plans for each of their lessons. Thus, asking for formal lesson plans, unless they are required to do so by their principals/districts, is asking teachers to do something many have not done since their certification programs, which for many, was their undergraduate experiences 20+ years prior . . . *teaching is an oral medium*—teachers can talk all day about what they are doing in their classes. Far fewer can, or have the time to write it out in sufficient detail for other people to follow.[4]

With this insight, other feedback secured from the evaluation, and advice from Dr. Christine Baron, we tried a new model of lesson plan creation that we called the Digital Hallway. We envisioned this as a place where teachers could share lesson ideas in short videos, much like in a hallway where teachers debrief and share ideas. Staff worked with the CT TOY council teachers to test and develop sample digital hallway videos. These samples and a template were shared with teachers on the first day of the three-day workshop. By sharing this concept and the instructions for it in the beginning hours of the program, teachers could immediately begin wrapping their heads around what they wanted to create and think about it as they approached each session, activity, or meeting with experts. The idea was that the teacher would make a two- to three-minute video explaining a lesson idea based on something at the museum that inspired them, incorporating existing resources from the MSE website. The video production for the Digital Hallway videos was completed in-house, and teachers filmed segments all over the museum grounds at spots relevant to their lesson ideas. We held daily check-in sessions where the cohort shared their thoughts and got feedback. By the end of the second day, each teacher submitted a brief proposal for their Digital Hallway lesson, including ideas on where to film and other details. This model has generated a significant number of videos to feature online and has proven a popular resource for educators to make and use. Mystic Seaport Museum has the advantage of a having a film and video studio with a dedicated staff person, but this concept can easily be modified and employed at other museums without those resources.

Other Essential Considerations for Teacher-Created Products

When embarking on any TPD program involving teacher-created products, here are some key considerations:

- *What experts will you involve in your project?* Make sure to enlist subject matter experts in your collaboration. Align teachers with these experts to create the content desired. Typically, curators, researchers, and museum teachers are good choices.
- *What resource types will you create?* In advance, decide on the materials to be created and instructions for participants. Will the resources be digital? Traditional lesson plans? Workshops for other educators? What templates will you provide?
- *How will you share the resources?* Consult with educators to decide on the best platform for sharing resources. Platforms do not have to be complicated. Use existing options that are easy to work with like your current website, YouTube, WordPress, Thinglink, or Google Classroom.
- *What will you do when teachers turn in their resources?* When the teacher hands in their resources, the real work begins. Who will copyedit materials and upload them to the preferred platform? Will all submitted projects be used?
- *How will you handle resource flops?* Not all teachers turn in usable projects. When running a TPD program in which teachers create materials, one should be prepared to deal with materials that do not get used. Any official program agreements should stipulate that teacher-created products will be published at the institution's discretion.
- *How will you compensate teachers for their contributions?* Teachers often feel underappreciated, so when they come to your museum to participate in TPD and create materials, they should be paid whenever possible, or, at minimum, recognized for their contributions.
- *How will you spread the word?* After your participants create materials, how will you get the word out? Will you host TPD sessions with your cocreating teachers to tell others about the materials and how to use them? Will you commission participants as ambassadors for your program?

While the teacher-created resources and models examined in this chapter might not fit your institution perfectly, aspects of each can be studied and reconfigured to work at many institutions. Look for inspirational projects for educators to be involved in at your site, ask them to help you create materials they will actually use, and hand over the reins to see what will happen. In addition, use evaluation techniques that work for your institution so you can better understand the needs of your program participants and the audience for your digital resources. Teacher-created education resources do not come without challenges but are worth the effort, leading to lasting relationships between teachers and museums and unique resources to aid student learning.

NOTES

1. Nina Simon, *The Participatory Museum* (Santa Cruz, CA: Museum 2.0, 2010), 3.
2. Christina O'Brien, interview by Krystal Rose, November 10, 2020.
3. Christina O'Brien, interview.
4. Krystal Kornegay Rose, Sarah Cahill, and Christine Baron, "Providing Teachers with What They Need: Re-Thinking Historic Site-Based Professional Development after Small-Scale Assessment," *Journal of Museum Education* 44, no. 2 (2019): 201–9, doi: 10.1080/10598650.2018.1539560.

10

Evaluation

Measuring Impact

Sarah Jencks

This chapter is an exploration of how a group of Washington, DC, historic sites has partnered to create long-standing teacher professional development institutes that center not only teacher learning but continuous learning and iteration on the part of the historic site staffs. The chapter is written from the perspective of staff at Ford's Theatre, the largest of the sites. Now more than ten years into the partnership, a single weeklong institute for local teachers has grown into two programs, one of which is repeated (for a total of three weeks of programming), as well as evening and weekend workshops offered throughout the year. First, we will look briefly at the structure and content of the institutes. Next, we will walk through the ways that staff—and, at times, outside contractors—collected and analyzed data. Last, we'll look at findings emerging from the evaluation and how they have supported the evolution of the teacher institutes and workshops. The goal is that you will come away with a sense of why program evaluation is worthwhile and at what level you want to do it.

Professional Development Collaborative as Professional Learning Community

The teacher professional development programs at Ford's Theatre aim to transform how teachers engage students in learning about the Civil War and its legacies. Specifically, Ford's Theatre seeks to challenge conceptions of Civil War history as a series of facts and dates about battles and military leaders, replacing them with a broader understanding of Civil War history as an engagement with places and artifacts, people and their stories, and enduring conflicts and tensions that can be made relevant to students' lives today. Additionally, Ford's Theatre and its historic site partners model the development of historical empathy and community building among teachers, both of which are instrumental to our approach to teaching history. Central to the approach is that the partners establish collegial norms and relationships that support innovative, creative, and relevant approaches to place-based history teaching. Ford's Theatre teacher professional development provides educators with access to historic sites, content area experts, and primary sources. The programs also draw on adult learning theory emphasizing communities of practice and reflection as integral to learning, and on pedagogies that center emotional engagement with places, people, artifacts, and events. The staff from the collaborating sites model the concepts of communities of practice and reflection in the implementation and evolution of the programs, which undergird the importance of the inquiry stance that supports our approach to evaluation.

The first summer institute, Civil War Washington, took place for DC-area teachers in 2008, with a second added in 2009 for teachers from around the country. The 2008 program was a collaborative effort by staff from Ford's Theatre, Tudor Place Historic House and Garden, the Frederick Douglass National Historic Site, and the National Mall and Memorial Parks, with President Lincoln's Cottage joining the effort in 2009. Our staffs have continued to work collaboratively every year since then, teaching the sites comparatively throughout the program week as a way to better impart the varied experiences of people living in Washington City during the war. In 2015, with support from the National Endowment for the Humanities' Landmarks in American History program, Ford's Theatre piloted a second institute intended to explore the aftermath of the Lincoln assassination and its effects on the country in the years that followed. As required by the Landmarks program, this institute included engagement with scholars, which Civil War Washington did not, and used places as a way to understand legacies and ideas.

In order to establish expectations and norms for each program, participants meet for dinner before the first full day of programs. At the dinner, the staff and participants introduce themselves, activating prior knowledge about the week's content and providing benchmarking for staff to know where each participant is beginning the week. In that first evening, participants go over the schedule for the week, discuss use of social media and expectations of what is shared and what is not ("What is said here stays here; what is learned here leaves here"), and get to know the Authentic Reflection prompts[1] and oral and written reflection tools that are used throughout the week to spur participant learning. The prompts are then used in oral reflections each morning and written throughout the week in a private online space that can be accessed throughout the following school year. This grounding work done on the first evening together is threaded through the whole week and beyond.

Collecting Annual Survey Data

Since the program's first year, staff have sent an online survey to institute participants in the late summer and again at the end of the school year, looking to understand their initial impressions of what they had learned and then to check in on how they had ultimately implemented and integrated what they learned into their classroom practice. These surveys asked participants to rate themselves on a range of knowledge, skills, and dispositions that the partners emphasized throughout the week of the institute, gauging their growth by asking for "before-the-institute" and "after-the-institute" ratings. The August survey items included everything from familiarity with Abraham Lincoln and Frederick Douglass to teaching with places and field trips to teaching close reading of historical speeches. Other survey questions included teachers' views on the usefulness of regular reflection prompts, both in writing and in person; thoughts on peer-to-peer learning, activity learning, and scholar/lecture learning, depending on the program; and speculation about what they were most likely to take back to their classrooms. The May survey was much shorter, asking participants to look back on the year and tell us what they had actually used or taught from the program, and what, after a year in the classroom, they saw as most valuable to themselves and to their practice.

Over the first five years of the program, we consistently got about 80 percent participation in the August survey and 50 percent participation in the May survey. The message from those who chose to participate was clear, though we were concerned the data was problematic because it was self-reported rather than demonstrated. Participants who completed the surveys were deeply enthusiastic about their experiences at the institute. They found the content to be compelling and, in many cases, new to them. They found the activities and practices to be transferable to their classrooms, and they found the collegiality among the participants to be uplifting. They also regularly noted how valued they felt and how grateful they were to be treated like professionals, which was sad but is worth noting.

This data was collected using SurveyMonkey, which allowed us to manipulate and analyze the data in some useful ways, including visualizing responses to questions asked with a Likert scale and creating word clouds to help surface trends in responses to open-ended questions. This diligent data collection and analysis was a great start, and it was helpful in giving us a sense of what was working and what we might want to tweak or even overhaul. At the end of our fifth program year, we sent out a survey to all five years' participants, and heard back from a solid 40 percent, telling us that they still valued their experience with the program. Many had built on their learning by attending other institutions' institutes or by becoming engaged with Ford's Theatre in one of our other programs. However, we wanted more and better information. The survey we created was adequate and helpful, but we didn't have the staff time to do a detailed analysis of the open-ended questions, and no one on our team had a doctorate in education or was steeped enough in educational research to help us determine which aspects of the programs were behind the positive feedback.

A Formal, External Evaluation

In 2016, Ford's Theatre received a multiyear grant from the Institute of Museum and Library Services' Museums for America program providing funding to conduct a two-year evaluation, with the intention of doing a rigorous, two-year evaluation of the programs. In order to learn from experts and get support in analyzing collected data, Ford's Theatre staff and collaborators partnered with Karen Kortecamp and Maia Sheppard, then both professors of education at George Washington University (Sheppard has since moved to the University of Iowa). We contacted them in 2015 and started working with them as part of the grant-writing process to design a comprehensive and thoughtful evaluation. Working with Kortecamp and Sheppard, who were recommended to us by the head of the university's museum education program, required us to articulate our intended learning objectives for the institute participants at a much finer grain than we had done in the past. Rather than following our instincts and designing our programs through discussion, our collaborators sat down together to spell out what we hoped the participants were taking away from their time with us. This process has had enormous value and allowed us to talk with teachers, school administrators, and funders about our work—even before we had collected and analyzed the data. By working with academic researchers who were already studying work with parallels to ours, we were able to keep our costs for evaluation to just over $15,000, spread over two years. Independent evaluators can be wonderful, and we have worked with many of them, but a benefit of academic partnerships like this, if you are able to secure one, is that they already have graduate research assistants and an interest in your work.

The evaluation design consisted of pre- and post-institute surveys, with participants looking at content knowledge, historical understanding, and what we called sense of efficacy, meaning how participants perceived their capacity to enact identified teaching practices like teaching with artifacts. We wrote open-ended content questions, which required that we then create open-ended answers to the questions that the scorers could use to compare to the participants' pre- and post-institute answers. Again, we learned a great deal from this process. The evaluators also held post-institute focus group discussions to investigate participants' experiences in a more open-ended way. Additionally, we asked participants to film themselves teaching part of a lesson at some point during the year that they felt reflected their learning from the institute, and to write a short reflection on the lesson and how it expressed what they had learned. We offered webinars during the school year after they participated on how to film themselves in the classroom and how to write reflectively about their teaching, in case they felt uncomfortable with either. The grant also allowed us to make the program free for participants in exchange for their participation in the data collection. We got full participation in the summer data collection and about 60 percent participation in the school-year data collection. To be clear, this data collection process was a lot of work, and it is not something we would recommend undertaking on a yearly basis.

The first-year evaluation affirmed our informal understandings about the institutes' outcomes. Data analysis found that participants left the one-week summer institutes with increased content knowledge and—frequently—changed and expanded historical understandings of the Civil War and its legacies, new strategies to teach about the same, and newly developed professional communities that could provide resources and support for their teaching. The use of teacher-filmed lessons was less effective, largely because the filming was unreliably useable, but the reflections the teachers wrote about teaching their lessons proved to be rich data for us and for Kortecamp and Sheppard to mine. These writings helped us understand the links between what we were modeling at the institute and what was actually happening in the participants' classrooms—and how we could make more explicit connections during the institute to make the transfer to the classroom smoother.

What Works

Feeling good about what we learned in our first year, we used the second year of evaluation to validate the findings from the first year, investigate which aspects of the programs were most effective and compelling for participants, and determine how we can best share what's working with the broader field. Our team collected the same data through the 2018 summer institutes. Kortecamp and Sheppard analyzed it and compared it to the 2017 data, and reported similar results.[2] At the same time, our evaluators helped us make connections between what they were identifying as most effective and research into identified "best" practices in adult and professional learning strategies.

The practices that Kortecamp and Sheppard identified as most compelling for and effective with teachers were consistent across both summers of data collection. They were not surprising, as they were the same things that we had heard about from participants anecdotally for years. These practices are situated learning, cultivating community, reflective practice, and historical empathy, and are aspects of experiential learning.[3] In their *Journal of Museum Education* article on their findings,[4] the researchers, writing with Ford's Theatre staff, explain the theoretical foundation of each of these practices and then connect them to the museum educators' practices. The researchers also noted, "Teachers described cross-organizational summer institute staff fostering this sense of community through structured discussions, creating a social atmosphere, treating teachers as professionals, and setting clear guidelines and expectations upfront."[5]

Situated learning takes place in an authentic setting rather than out of context. Kortecamp and Sheppard use the work of cultural and social anthropologist Jean Lave to explain, "What is learned cannot be separated from where learning takes place and who participates in the learning experiences." Dialogic tours, direct interactions with documents and objects, and centering first-person accounts are all ways to enact situated learning. However, situated learning must be accompanied by reflection.

Reflective practice means that after—or during—learning experiences, we intentionally create time for learners to reflect, whether orally, in writing, or silently. This reflection might take place immediately, but accommodating learners who need more time to process might mean doing so the next morning or offering an online platform for reflecting at home in the evening. This practice harkens back to the granddaddy of educational philosophy, John Dewey, who is famously—and spuriously—quoted, in what should be a paraphrase, as writing that one does not learn from experience; one learns by reflecting upon experience. Somewhat more recently, philosopher Donald Schön posited similar ideas in his book, *The Reflective Practitioner: How Professionals Think in Action.*[6]

Cultivating community is crucial to making a learning space that acknowledges the experience and wisdom that participants bring to it. By asking participants to bring their full selves into the rooms where we learn—be they historic, virtual, or otherwise—and encouraging them to learn from one another as much as from the group leaders and scholars, we draw on the work of Etienne Wenger.[7] He describes learning as "social participation" and originated the idea of "communities of practice." We begin the work of cultivating community in the institute application by asking what an applicant believes they will bring to the institute—

and what they will take from it. It requires getting to know participants through their applications and by listening carefully and asking about regional and personal differences during the course of the program. Ask participants how they might be able to transfer what they're learning, what barriers they see, and what questions they have.

Historical empathy is crucial. Social studies education researchers Jason Endacott and Sarah Brooks describe historical empathy as three interrelated and interdependent factors: historical contextualization, perspective taking, and affective connection. Sheppard and Kortecamp explain the three factors, quoting Endacott and Brooks:

> Historical contextualization requires a deep understanding of a time period, its social, cultural, and political norms, and knowledge of events that led up to "the historical situation." Perspective-taking requires "understanding of another's prior lived experience, principles, positions, attitudes, and beliefs in order to understand how that person might have thought about the situation in question." Affective connection requires "consideration for how historical figures' lived experiences, situations, or actions may have been influenced by the affective response based on a connection made to one's own similar yet different life experience." They suggest a four-phase model to promote historical empathy to scaffold learners' thinking that begins with introducing the historical situation, followed by an historical inquiry, then a display of what has been learned, and finally, reflection to make connections explicit.[8]

By diving deeply into the experiences of individuals, and their relationships to words in documents, and with the use or creation of objects, participants build affective connections that they then share with their students.

A Layered or Tiered Approach to Evaluation

Ford's Theatre extended its engagement with Kortecamp and Sheppard for one more year, finishing up its grant project by sharing findings at meetings like the American Association for State and Local History and the National Council for the Social Studies. Creating these presentations forced staff and evaluators to synthesize what we learned and to share it in ways that are meaningful to fellow practitioners. The evaluation process has made it possible for us to talk about our work in a wider context of research and theory across disciplines and to explain it to school administrators and funders in ways we couldn't previously. That said, we have returned to simpler evaluation strategies. We still ask participants to respond to surveys at the end of each session, and we ask them again in May. We want to make sure our programs are relevant and compelling, but now we feel confident in our pedagogies and content choices. There are a wide variety of ways to do evaluation, and each institution needs to decide from year to year on its goals and needs and design evaluation tools and plans accordingly.

NOTES

1. Abby Remer, "Authentic Reflection," page on Remer's education consultancy website, Abby Remer, Education Consultant (1996–2009), http://www.virtualforum.com/aremer/authenticreflection.cfm.
2. Karen Kortecamp and Maia Sheppard, "Ford's Theatre (and Partners) Summer Teacher Institutes, 2016 and 2017: An Evaluation Report" (Washington, DC: Ford's Theatre Society, 2018), https://fords-theatre.s3.amazonaws.com/files/resources/fts-teaching-fellow-evaluation-report-summary-2018.pdf.
3. Lee Andresen, David Boud, and Ruth Cohen, "Experience-Based Learning," in *Understanding Adult Education and Training*, ed. Griff Foley, second edition (St. Leonards, Australia: Allen & Unwin, 2000), 225–39.
4. Maia Sheppard, Karen Kortecamp, Sarah Jencks, Jake Flack, and Alexandria Wood, "Connecting Theory and Practice: Using Place-Based Learning in Teacher Professional Development," *Journal of Museum Education* 44, no. 2 (2019): 187–200, https://doi.org/10.1080/10598650.2019.1597598.
5. Sheppard, Kortecamp, et al., "Connecting Theory and Practice," p. 190.
6. Donald Schön posited similar ideas in his book, *The Reflective Practitioner: How Professionals Think in Action* (New York: Basic Books, 1984).
7. Etienne Wenger-Trayner and Beverly Wenger-Trayner's consultancy website and blog, https://wenger-trayner.com/.
8. Sheppard, Kortecamp, et al., "Connecting Theory and Practice."

11

✢

Implementing
Evaluation Findings

Lora Cooper and Krystal Rose

Like many institutions, Mystic Seaport Museum and Monticello have hosted various types of teacher professional development (TPD) programs for decades. To evaluate the programs, we have frequently employed traditional Likert scale surveys to give us the basic details of teachers' reactions to our programming. Essentially, we discovered whether or not teachers like the programs or whether their feelings fell somewhere in between. The responses typically gave us enough information to decide if we should do a program again, and some encouraging quotes to share with stakeholders, but did not give us the constructive feedback we needed to reorient our programming around the needs of our participants.[1]

In 2014, we joined together with researchers from Teachers College, Columbia University, and Tufts University to complete an evaluation using Q-Methodology, supported by an Institute of Museum and Library Services National Leadership Grant Project. Q-Methodology was used to assess:

1. The Monticello Teacher Institute (MTI) in 2016, 2017, and 2018;
2. The Connecticut Teacher of the Year (CT TOY) program at Mystic Seaport Museum in 2017 and 2018;
3. The Mystic Seaport for Educators (MSE) Summer Fellows Program in 2017 and 2018; and
4. The Mount Vernon for Teachers Summer Teacher Institute in 2018.

After careful study by the project researchers and museum education staff, the results were used to restructure future TPD programs. While the assessment offered the certainty of quantitative data, some of the most valuable insights came from the interviews conducted as part of the evaluation, adding a qualitative level of detail. The evaluation revealed patterns in participating teachers' thinking and learning. Being able to see how teachers' understandings of history shifted, revealed what we had, or had not, accomplished. This chapter reviews the concrete, often simple adjustments made to the Mystic Seaport Museum and Monticello programs that the evaluation proved to be effective improvements, therefore demonstrating the value of implementing the study.

About the Programs

Monticello Teacher Institute

The Monticello Teacher Institute is a weeklong program hosted at Monticello, including both the historic plantation and the Jefferson Library at the International Center for Jefferson Studies. Originally funded out of a research fellowship, the program asks teachers to create classroom resources while receiving a comprehensive overview of the history of Monticello, from nation-building to enslavement to architecture. Intended to draw teachers from around the country, the program encourages participants to become ambassadors as their work is shared on the Monticello Digital Classroom website.

The Connecticut Teachers of the Year Program

The CT TOY program is a three-day program where the cohort of CT TOY finalists experience a "buffet" of content and activities at Mystic Seaport Museum. Participants tour the campus, experience behind-the-scenes tours of the collection vaults, climb the rigging of our historic ships, experience primary source workshops, and attend lectures given by experts. The program ended with time spent creating lesson plans for the MSE website. Over the years we had been hosting the program, the number of lesson plans turned in had been dwindling.

Mystic Seaport for Educators Summer Fellows Program

We also evaluated the MSE Summer Fellows program, which focuses on developing teacher-created resources to be featured on the MSE website. Participants take part in a suite of on-site orientation workshops, including collections tours, one-on-one meetings with curators, writing workshops, and brainstorming sessions with staff and other educators. They then create their own flexible summer schedules and come to the museum to do research, brainstorm with others, and check in with staff. Participants share their projects in a presentation at the end of the summer and, eventually, their work is featured on the website.

Lessons Revealed

Accepting Our Roles as Teacher Educators

While some museums and institutions might have the luxury of professionally trained and experienced teacher educators on staff, many do not. Those of us leading TPDs are most often museum professionals with expertise in our content, not teacher education. If pedagogy is something teachers want support in through TPD, museum educators need to receive training on the pedagogical methods, theories, and current research about teaching. Engaging with the field of TPD and learning the professional standards through the creation and implementation of this evaluation was instrumental in reframing our understanding of teachers as an audience and our roles and capacity to facilitate their learning. Understandably so, our original thinking was internally focused: Wouldn't teachers be thrilled to learn about all our resources, and wouldn't it reflect well on us to have teacher-created resources on our website? They are, and it does. But both of those aims are actually strengthened by slowing down to understand what is most valuable to teacher learning and how to facilitate transference to the classroom. We now have fewer content presentations on our program schedules to have greater influence.

Know Your Participants and Meet Their Needs

The evaluation revealed that our participants were seeking distinct outcomes in each of our programs. In some cases, we met their articulated needs, and in others, we fell flat. For example, the MSE fellows were interested in pedagogical strategy, historical thinking skills, and Mystic Seaport Museum content development. The Q-sort results indicated that the experience met expectations for most participants, likely because the Fellows program was flexible and gave opportunities for the participants to seek out the things that interested them. In the Q-sort interviews, several fellows shared their desire to spend more time learning to do research and having the time to do it. After all, they are expected to model this for their students. By the end of the fellowship, some participants shared that they achieved this personal and professional goal through the program. This information taught us the importance of the pre-TPD interview or questionnaire: we now ask questions of the teachers at the beginning of each program, then make manageable accommodations and changes based on needs and expectations. While this is not a formal evaluation on the same scale as using Q-Methodology, the pre-program interview is an easy and worthwhile practice we can sustainably implement moving forward.

At Monticello, the evaluation revealed a consistent desire among teachers to take home resources that would help them teach both the content and skills of history. Therefore, following our own goals and norms-setting session, we now include a session titled "What Is History?," originally developed by colleagues for training our frontline interpreters. Equipping teachers with a clear framework for both creating resources and understanding the work of public history has resulted in richer conversations and more engaging classroom activities that align with skills-based standards.

Modify the "Buffet" Approach

For years, the CT TOY program was based on the idea that teachers need to experience a little bit of *everything* we have to offer at the museum, from lectures and tours to experiences like rowing a whaleboat or climbing the rigging. The Q-sort helped us understand that this is the opposite of what teachers wanted. CT TOY participants expressed that there was little time for deep exploration and digestion and that the program activities were often overwhelming. As a result, we made two significant changes to the program: offering fewer things in greater depth and letting the teachers determine some element of what they are doing.

One of the simplest yet most radical examples of this at Monticello is how we schedule the sessions within our program. In 2016, we took our teachers on a Hemings Family Tour on the fourth afternoon of the program as the last event of the day. This tour examines some of Monticello's most complex history and its legacies related to race, power, gender, and more in America today. And yet at the conclusion, we simply sent them off on their own for the evening! It also derailed several teachers' projects fairly late in the week, as it enlightened them to stories and perspectives they had not yet had a chance to consider. So in 2017, we moved the tour to the second morning of the program and followed it with a debrief conversation on how to share challenging narratives with students. This so radically changed the teachers' experience with our site that upon reviewing the initial evaluation data, Dr. Baron called and asked, "What did you do?" The answer was as simple as a little scheduling. In 2021, a staffing challenge revealed a new opportunity to offer our pedagogical sessions on teaching complex history in the morning before the tour and the accompanying debrief in the afternoon. This gave our teachers both the time and the tools to process the content for themselves so that they could then translate it into knowledge for their students.

Collaboration and Professional Networks

The evaluation revealed to us that one of the most important aspects of TPD is collaborating and bouncing ideas off peers. Participants prioritized statements in the Q-sort concourse related to spending time and networking with like-minded peers and receiving constructive feedback from peers. Adding these sessions into our programs complemented our other significant change of doing fewer things in greater depth.

While networking time might appear superfluous to fulfilling program objectives when examining the schedule, it often takes the form of a happy hour or catered dinner. MTI has also implemented formal means for collaboration, such as project check-in groups to support their fellow educators' resource development throughout the week. However, unstructured opportunities are just as significant to supporting their professional learning. Teachers come to sites for growth but also refreshment; evaluation revealed how they often don't have strong support networks in their own schools, especially ones specific to their area of social studies. In recent years, they have taught through contentious elections, a civil rights movement, and global crises in addition to the everyday challenges of curriculum standards and school administrations. Giving teachers space to vent, compare, and bolster one another cannot be underestimated in value, as it releases them to focus on the opportunities before them and sends them back to their classrooms newly inspired.

Achievable and Useful Teacher-Created Products

An issue we ran into almost every year of the CT TOY program was that our participants were overwhelmed not only by the amount of content and the number of activities in the programming, but also by our asking them to make lesson plans. Our evaluation researchers suggested that we revise the "final product" assignment and reminded us that teaching is an oral medium. With this in mind, we opted for a new type of lesson plan: video lesson plans we now call the "Digital Hallway." These two-to-five-minute videos feature participants sharing a lesson or activity idea. Teachers have responded favorably to the implementation of the Digital Hallway and created some exciting content, which is also more popular with the educators using our digital resources. Re-read chapter 11 for more on teacher-created products.

Exploring Pedagogy and Content Simultaneously

The Q-sort taught us that our CT TOY program participants learned a lot about our museum's content, but not so much about pedagogy. That information helped us shift our content delivery and use the content as an opportunity to examine or demonstrate appropriate pedagogical concepts. While our content is important, what is even more critical for this audience is *how to teach it*. One small change we made to answer the need for pedagogical instruction is the addition of a workshop focused on reading and understanding historical documents. The workshop uses both our incredible manuscript collection and helps teachers develop conceptual threads that tie back to their classroom work. At Monticello, teachers participate in some of the same activities used with school programs, letting them learn about the legacies of the Declaration of Independence and daily life for different individuals across the plantation. They then discuss questions like: How would you use this? What would you add? What historical concepts does it convey?

While such an intensive evaluation is not feasible, or sustainable, for a majority of institutions, we recommend the following steps to use evaluation in strengthening your own TPD:

1. Use the lessons we learned in our evaluation in your program. Because the analysis was based on national standards for teacher education and history education, these same takeaways should bolster the influence of your programming and demonstrate the significance of TPD at historic sites and museums to your stakeholders.
2. Implement whatever degree of evaluation you can. While it may be as simple as an exit survey you build for yourself in Google Forms or SurveyMonkey, create opportunities to listen to educators, reflect on your program, and consider your institutional objectives and their alignment with the principles of andragogy and classroom education.
3. Connect with professional teacher educators. Beyond the findings, our relationships with our researchers from the field of formal education have been the greatest boon to our programs in strengthening our understanding of teacher learning and needs. Reach out to teacher certification programs at nearby colleges to see how your work can be mutually beneficial.

Find the full analysis and development of this evaluation at teacherin sites.org.

Find a full list of resources dedicated to evaluation and research on teacherinsites.org, including videos and references detailing the intricacies of Q-Methodology. You'll even find an adaptable version of the 2018 concourse used at Monticello, Mount Vernon, and Mystic Seaport Museum. While the full analysis may not be feasible for your institution, it offers an insightful reflection activity for participants and reminder of the field standards of teacher learning and history education.

NOTE

1. Krystal Kornegay Rose, Sarah Cahill, and Christine Baron, "Providing Teachers with What They Need: Re-thinking Historic Site-based Professional Development After Small-Scale Assessment," *Journal of Museum Education* 44, no. 2 (2019): 201.

Appendix 1

Logistical Tips and Tricks

Maslow's hierarchy of needs has often helped us consider the practicalities of offering effective teacher professional development at historic sites and museums. Once you have established program objectives based on the professional needs of teachers, what are the base layers that support a successful TPD that affirms teachers and achieves its goals? Here is a list of suggestions and considerations to help meet the physical and personal needs of participants, developed by museum educators at the Summit on Teacher Professional Development at Historic Sites and Museums held at Mount Vernon in September 2019.

1. Overcommunicate: This applies to every element of a program, from confirming receipt of an application to sending out letters of completion after the program. Clear expectations upon arrival helps set teachers at ease and maintaining that communication helps shift between sessions and activities.
2. Use your program itinerary—don't worship it. If your participants vocalize a need or interest, see if you can make it happen. It's often as simple as delaying a session fifteen minutes for an extra break but may mean reorganizing the next day to provide access to additional resources.
   - When drafting your itinerary, calculate how many hours are spent on content, pedagogy, reflection, content creation, and socializing respectively to make sure you keep the balance you're aiming for.

- Allow for plenty of breaks. One option is to list sessions that are intended to be forty-five minutes as an hour long so that you have breathing room for bathroom breaks or overflow questions.
- Consider the weather. It may seem self-evident but scheduling outdoor sessions for the hottest or predictably stormy times of day comes at a cost. Whenever possible, have alternative plans or locations reserved. Whether or not you set a program dress code, let them know what kind of conditions to expect; it's hard to think when you're shivering in a climate-controlled museum gallery.

3. Accessibility: Ask your teachers in advance how you can help them participate successfully. If your historic site has inherent limitations, such as stairs or uneven pathways, make sure teachers are aware. Do presenters need amplification? Is seating available along the routes of walking tours? Make sure participants know they can ask a staff member privately if a challenge arises.

4. Workspace: Is your primary meeting space large enough for everyone to be comfortable? Is it configured to allow for interaction and presentations? Are there sufficient nearby restrooms and water fountains?
   - If your session is virtual, have you checked to make sure everyone can access the platform? Dedicate staff roles to managing the waiting room, breakout rooms, screen sharing, and muting participants as necessary.

5. Materials: Be ready for interactive sessions and to support teacher-created products. There should be pens and notebooks as well as outlets and Wi-Fi to facilitate different modalities. Know how you'll share printed and digital materials and how you'll ask teachers to submit their work.

6. Refreshments: Never underestimate the value of a snack basket. Check with participants in advance about dietary restrictions and make a variety of snacks consistently available. This helps everyone take care of their individual needs and makes teachers feel valued and welcome.
   - For multiday programs, set expectations with teachers about breakfasts, lunches, and dinners. If budgeting allows, provide a stipend to cover the meals that are not included in the program. Provided meals can double as discussion sessions or networking opportunities.

7. Transportation: If you're running a multiday program or visiting multiple sites, can you provide transportation? If you're asking teachers to carpool, can you reimburse for mileage? Share directions and parking instructions on paper and digitally.

8. Accommodations: Providing accommodations is the most expensive element of a multiday program aside from travel. Partnerships with

local universities or negotiated discounts with a hotel can help mitigate costs. While asking teachers to share rooms can cut costs further, they far prefer to have their own space (especially in light of ongoing COVID-19 concerns at the time of authorship).

9. Financial arrangements: A refundable deposit can help ensure attendance.
10. Norm setting and cohort development: Making a disparate group of teachers into a cohort takes effort. In proportion to the length of your program, set aside time to communicate norms and expectations. A virtual session may just need one slide to set expectations for what you'll cover and when you'll take questions, but a weeklong program benefits from a teambuilding activity you can refer to in future dialogic sessions.
11. Staffing: Make sure your participants know who to contact on a given day or about a given issue. Consider naming someone to be "on call" each day of a weeklong program so that staff members can attend to other responsibilities.
12. Stakeholders: Invite members of your institution's development team and current or potential donors to attend a particularly captivating session of your program to garner support and demonstrate the work they make possible.
13. Photography: Take both candid and formal group photos of every session. Whether you contract a professional for a couple of hours or have an intern standby with the latest iPhone, dedicate this task to someone who is not also running the program. This will give you refreshed material for promoting the program and sharing with stakeholders.
14. Recognition: Show your appreciation for participants and session presenters; a little pomp and circumstance shows teachers just how awesome you think they are. Ask teachers to sign thank you notes for the staff who work with them.
15. Enjoy being with enthusiastic educators!

Reach out through the Teacher InSites Collaborative to see how colleagues plan and prepare for different programs. Taking care of your teachers and your program staff will let everyone involved focus on the learning at hand.

+

Appendix 2
A Note about Scaling and Funding

Many of the programs described throughout this volume are dependent upon dedicated funding made possible by grants, endowments, and donations supported by the institutions' development teams. Hosting a weeklong summer program is expensive, especially when travel and lodging are provided. Part of our purpose in publishing this book is to offer institutions the evidence and intellectual resources to solicit the support required to create the ideal program. Teachers and students are a moving audience for donors, and we hope this research, in addition to wonderful teacher quotes and photographs, bring stakeholders on board. If new to offering teacher professional development, start small. Look for partnerships with your local school districts or other museums. Offer virtual sessions that can stand alone or a half-day, in-person session. We look forward to success stories from across the field of museum educators offering their very best for classroom teachers.

Index

About the Contributors

Mike Adams, Museum and Audience Engagement Director, Hagley Museum and Library

CherylAnne Amendola, Teacher, Montclair Kimberly Academy

Dina A. Bailey, Mountain Top Vision Consulting

Christine Baron, Assistant Professor of Social Studies and Education, Teachers College, Columbia University

Melanie Bowyer, Manager of Digital Media and Strategy, Monticello

Kristen D. Burton, Assistant Lecturer, Department of History and Classics, University of Alberta

Alysha Butler-Arnold, Teacher, African American History and US History, McKinley Technology High School

Lora Cooper, Continuing Education Coordinator, Monticello

Georgette Hackman, Teacher, Cocalico Middle School

Sarah Jencks, Partner, The History Co:Lab

Jacqueline Langholtz, Development Officer, Monticello

Karen Richey, History and Social Science Teacher, Toby Johnson Middle School

Krystal Rose, Curator of Collections, Mystic Seaport Museum

Stephanie van Hover, Professor and Department Chair of Curriculum, Instruction, and Special Education, School of Education and Human Development, University of Virginia

Rob Wallace, STEM Education Specialist, National WWII Museum

Allison Wickens, Vice President for Education, Mount Vernon